MIDDLE GRADES MATHEMATICS PROJECT

Mouse and Elephant: Measuring Growth

Janet Shroyer

William Fitzgerald

Addison-Wesley Publishing Company

Menlo Park, California • Reading, Massachusetts • Don Mills, Ontario
Wokingham, England • Amsterdam • Sydney • Singapore
Tokyo • Mexico City • Bogotá • Santiago • San Juan

This book is published by the Addison-Wesley Innovative Division.

The blackline masters in this publication are designed to be used with appropriate duplicating equipment to reproduce copies for classroom use. Addison-Wesley Publishing Company grants permission to classroom teachers to reproduce these masters.

ISBN 0-201-21474-1

13 14 15 - ML - 95 94 93

About the authors

William Fitzgerald, Ph.D. in mathematics education, University of Michigan, joined the faculty of Michigan State University in 1966 and has been Professor of Mathematics and Education since 1971. He has had extensive experience at all levels of mathematics teaching and has been involved in the development of mathematics laboratories.

Glenda Lappan, B.A., Mercer University, Macon, Georgia, and Ed.D., University of Georgia, is Professor of Mathematics at Michigan State University. She directed the mathematics component of MSU Sloan Foundation Minority Engineering Project. She has taught high school mathematics and since 1976 has worked regularly with students and teachers of grades 3–8.

Elizabeth Phillips, B.S. in mathematics and chemistry, Wisconsin State University, and M.S. in mathematics, University of Notre Dame, was visiting scholar in mathematics education at Cambridge University, England. She conducts inservice workshops for teachers and is the author of several papers and books. Currently she is a faculty member in the Department of Mathematics at Michigan State University.

Janet Shroyer, B.S., Knox College, and Ph.D., Michigan State University, has taught mathematics in Lansing public schools and at Oregon College of Education. She was a consultant in the Office of Research Services, evaluator of a teacher corps project, and a research intern in the Institute for Research on Teaching. Presently she is Associate Professor in the Mathematics Department of Aquinas College, Grand Rapids, Michigan.

Mary Jean Winter, A.B., Vassar College, and Ph.D. in mathematics, Carnegie Institute of Technology, has been Professor of Mathematics at Michigan State University since 1965. She has been involved in mathematics education at both school and college (teacher training) level since 1975. She has been especially interested in developing middle school and secondary activities using computers and other manipulatives.

A special note of recognition

Sincere appreciation is expressed to the following persons for their significant contribution to the Middle Grades Mathematics Project.

Assistants:	**David Ben-Haim**
	Alex Friedlander
	Zaccheaus Oguntebi
	Patricia Yarbrough
Consultant for evaluation:	**Richard Shumway**
Consultants for development:	**Keith Hamann**
	John Wagner

Contents

MIDDLE GRADES MATHEMATICS PROJECT
Mouse and Elephant: Measuring Growth

Mouse and Elephant: Measuring Growth

The Middle Grades Mathematics Project (MGMP) is a curriculum program developed at Michigan State University funded by the National Science Foundation to develop units of high quality mathematics instruction for grades 5 through 8. Each unit

- is based on a related collection of important mathematical ideas
- provides a carefully sequenced set of activities that leads to an understanding of the mathematical challenges
- helps the teacher foster a problem-solving atmosphere in the classroom
- uses concrete manipulatives where appropriate to help provide the transition from concrete to abstract thinking
- utilizes an instructional model that consists of three phases: launch, explore, and summarize
- provides a carefully developed instructional guide for the teacher
- requires two to three weeks of instructional time

The goal of the MGMP materials is to help students develop a deep, lasting understanding of the mathematical concepts and strategies studied. Rather than attempting to break the curriculum into small bits to be learned in isolation from each other, MGMP materials concentrate on a cluster of important ideas and the relationships that exist among these ideas. Where possible the ideas are embodied in concrete models to assist students in moving from the concrete stage to more abstract reasoning.

THE INSTRUCTIONAL MODEL: LAUNCH, EXPLORE, AND SUMMARIZE

Many of the activities in the MGMP are built around a specific mathematical challenge. The instructional model used in all five units focuses on helping students solve the mathematical challenge. The instruction is divided into three phases.

During the first phase the teacher *launches* the challenge. The launching consists of introducing new concepts, clarifying definitions, reviewing old concepts, and issuing the challenge.

The second phase of instruction is the class *exploration*. During exploration, students work individually or in small groups. Students may be gathering data, sharing ideas, looking for patterns, making conjectures, or developing other types of problem-solving strategies. It is inevitable that students will exhibit variation in progress. The teacher's role during exploration is to move about the classroom, observing individual performances and encouraging on-task behavior. The teacher urges students to persevere in seeking a solution to the challenge. The teacher does this by asking appropriate questions and by providing confirmation and redirection where needed. For the more able students, the teacher provides extra challenges related to the ideas

Introduction

being studied. The extent to which students require attention will vary, as will the nature of attention they need, but the teacher's continued presence and interest in what they are doing is critical.

When most of the students have gathered sufficient data, they return to a whole class mode (often beginning the next day) for the final phase of instruction, *summarizing*. Here the teacher has an opportunity to demonstrate ways to organize data so that patterns and related rules become more obvious. Discussing the strategies used by students helps the teacher to guide them in refining these strategies into efficient, effective problem-solving techniques.

The teacher plays a central role in this instructional model. The teacher provides and motivates the challenge and then joins the students in exploring the problem. The teacher asks appropriate questions, encouraging and redirecting where needed. Finally, through the summary, the teacher helps students to deepen their understanding of both the mathematical ideas involved in the challenge and the strategies used to solve it.

To aid the teacher in using the instructional model, a detailed instructional guide is provided for each activity. The preliminary pages contain a rationale; an overview of the main ideas; goals for the students; and a list of materials and worksheets. Then a script is provided to help the teacher teach each phase of the instructional model. Each page of the script is divided into three columns:

TEACHER ACTION	TEACHER TALK	EXPECTED RESPONSE
This column includes materials used, what to display on the overhead, when to explain a concept, when to ask a question, etc.	This column includes important questions and explanations that are needed to develop understandings and problem-solving skills, etc.	This column includes correct responses as well as frequent incorrect responses and suggestions for handling them.

Worksheet answers, when appropriate, and review problem answers are provided at the end of each unit; and for each unit test, an answer key and a blackline master answer sheet is included.

RATIONALE

Students are not adequately learning measurement concepts, let alone the more important relationships between measurements. Evidence of this continues to accumulate from a variety of sources including the National Assessment of Educational Progress (NAEP). Students' incorrect responses and the nature of their errors to relatively simple questions involving area, perimeter, surface area, and volume continue to dismay those who examine test results.

Students tend to think of measurement concepts in terms of formulas rather than the number of units needed to cover or fill a given object. For example, area is typically thought of as length times width and not as the number of squares or other units that exactly cover a

Introduction

shape. Terms often are not associated with correct concepts. To a question about perimeter, students may respond with the area. Incorrect counting strategies may be used to count the number of units of measure. Perimeter may be found by counting the outer squares, and volume may be found by looking at a picture of a solid shape and counting only the visible squares or cubes.

Students able to answer questions about particular measures are often unaware of important relationships. Knowing the effect of varying arrangements when one measure is held constant is rare. For example, students may not realize how area will change in accordance with shape while perimeter remains constant. Despite their importance, the effects of growth on the measures of a shape or solid are not usually learned in school.

Interpreters of the results of tests and research tasks indicating students' lack of knowledge of measurement tend to focus on the same problems. Measurement is taught primarily from textbooks that focus on rules and rely on pictures. Students need to have concrete learning tasks, not simply for motivation or introduction but for continued exploration of interesting ideas. The Mouse and Elephant unit provides students with hands-on experiences to explore measurement concepts and relationships.

UNIT OVERVIEW

In the Mouse and Elephant unit the concepts of area, perimeter, surface area, and volume are introduced with tiles, cubes, and story language. Explorations of different topics throughout the unit encourage students to discover important rules and relationships. The unit challenge is designed to motivate students to answer two fairly sophisticated and difficult questions: Given a mouse and an elephant of specified heights, how many mice does it take to balance the elephant, and how many mouse coats are needed to make a coat for the elephant?

Area and perimeter are first encountered in Activity 1 with the use of tiles. The story line concerns the use of small square tables arranged into rectangular banquet tables. Area is determined by the number of small tables that comprise the banquet table; perimeter is conveyed by the number of people able to sit at the banquet table if four people can be seated at a small table. The concepts of surface area and volume are introduced in Activity 4. Using cubes to represent food for travel in space, students make packages and cover them with space armor jackets. The number of days the food supply will last is the volume, and the cost of a space armor jacket at $1 per square is the surface area.

Examining the effects of holding one measure constant and varying the shape, as well as determining which shapes produce the maximum and minimum values in the varying measures, are the basic tasks of four activities. In Activity 2 students form rectangles with the same area and study the consequences on perimeter. The reverse task, which holds perimeter constant and allows area to vary, is the challenge of Activity 3. Similarly, in Activity 5 volume remains constant while students explore the effects of varying shape on surface area. They reverse this task in Activity 6, complicated by the imposition of a maximum surface area and minimum volume, which requires the introduction of a comparative measure—the cost per cube.

Introduction

Throughout these activities students gather sufficient data from which to recognize rules for finding measures, as well as to determine the relationships involving shape and maximum and minimum values of the varying measures.

In the last two activities, the effects of growth on different measures are investigated. In Activity 7 students determine the effects of growing squares, squares with changing edges, on the perimeter and area. The impact of growing edges on cubes is found for surface area and volume in Activity 8. At the culmination of this last activity, students solve the unit challenges: They find how many mouse coats are needed to sew a coat for the elephant and how many mice are needed to balance the elephant.

The tiles used in this unit are 1-inch square ceramic tiles that can be obtained from a local tile store. Soak the sheets in hot water to remove the backing, rinse, dry, and package in zip-lock plastic bags, 24 to a bag, plus a few extras, for each student. If you cannot get 1-inch tiles, you will need to change the scale on the figures from the student worksheets for Activity 1. Tiles are used in Activities 1, 2, 3, and 7.

The cubes should be 2 cm on an edge and can be wooden or plastic. For any other size you will need to change the 2-cm square paper and the jackets on Worksheet 4-2. Package 24 cubes of the same color, plus a few extras, for each student.

Activity A

UNIT CHALLENGE

OVERVIEW

The Mouse and Elephant unit is carefully designed and sequenced to convey the mathematical concepts and relationships necessary to solve the unit challenge. The challenge is intended to help motivate students to pursue the solution and to provide them with an opportunity to apply their new knowledge to real though fanciful problems dealing with the effect of growth on volume and surface area.

The unit challenge asks, "How many mouse coats are needed to sew a coat for the elephant?" and "How many mice are needed on the scales to balance the elephant?" The only information supplied is that the mouse stands 6 cm tall and the elephant 240 cm tall. During the unit, students will make and use jackets that cover packages of cubes. The solutions can be found by realizing that an elephant is really just a large mouse; each is in the shape of a cube; and their weights are comparable for the same volume. Thus, the elephant must be viewed as being 40 times as large as the mouse in linear dimension in order to apply the rules of growth that emerge in the last activity: As the edge grows by n, the surface area grows by n squared and the volume by n cubed.

Few students in the middle grades can be expected to have the knowledge or maturity to think about these questions effectively before completing the activities. Nevertheless, it is important for students to predict the solution in order to focus on its nature. Predictions can be kept confidential: have students place all their work in large envelopes during the unit, or collect their work without indicating the correctness of the predictions. Students should be encouraged to adjust and resubmit their predictions as the unit unfolds and they gain more insight into the problem.

One of the blackline masters contains 9 squares, each with a picture of a mouse that is 6 cm tall. Copying this sheet will provide enough mice to cut and tape a strip that is 40 mice tall. By folding this 40-mouse strip in an accordion-fashion beforehand, a single mouse can be displayed before you unfold it to produce a mouse measure of the elephant's height. By leaving the mouse strip taped on the wall during the unit, students will be reminded of the questions and can refer to it whenever the unit problem arises.

Goals for students

I. Make at least one written guess for the Mouse and Elephant questions (the unit challenge).

Materials

Mouse and Elephant Challenge and Guess Sheet (Materials A-1).

40-mouse strip, precut, taped, and folded (Materials A-2).

TEACHER ACTION	TEACHER TALK	EXPECTED RESPONSE
Distribute Mouse and Elephant Challenge and Guess Sheet (Materials A-1) for students to read.	In the Mouse and Elephant, your challenge is to answer two questions by the time we have completed the unit. The questions have to do with a mouse that is 6 cm tall and an elephant that is 240 cm tall. The questions are:	
Tell the story and pose the challenge.	How many mouse coats are needed to sew a coat for the elephant?	
	How many mice are needed on the scales to balance the elephant?	
	In order to find the answers, assume that this elephant is really just a large mouse. How many mouse coats do you think it takes to make the elephant's coat? How many mice does it take to balance the elephant?	Various answers, including 40.
After answers have been offered, including 40, ask.	The answer of 40 has been given. Where did the 40 come from?	$40 \times 6 = 240$ or $240 \div 6 = 40$
	How does the 40 relate to the mouse and elephant?	The elephant is the height of 40 mice.
Display one mouse (Materials A-2) and ask.	This is a picture of a mouse 6 cm high. How tall would the elephant be if the elephant were here in our classroom?	Various answers. Have students tell where on the wall the elephant comes.
After guesses are made, tape the 40-mouse strip to the wall.		
Point to the strip and ask.	Our 40-mouse strip shows how tall our elephant really is. Will 40 mice balance the elephant? Will the cloth from the coats of 40 mice be enough to make a coat for the elephant?	No; no.
Ask and let students record. Collect students' guess sheets.	On your guess sheet, record your guesses for the number of mouse coats needed to sew a coat for the elephant and the number of mice needed to balance the elephant.	

Mouse & Elephant Unit Challenge

The mouse stands 6 cm high and the elephant stands 240 cm high.

How many mouse coats are needed to sew a coat for the elephant?

How many mice are needed on the scales to balance the elephant?

Mouse & Elephant Guess Sheet

The number of mouse coats needed to sew a coat for the elephant is _____.

The number of mice needed on the scales to balance the elephant is _____.

Name _____ Date _____

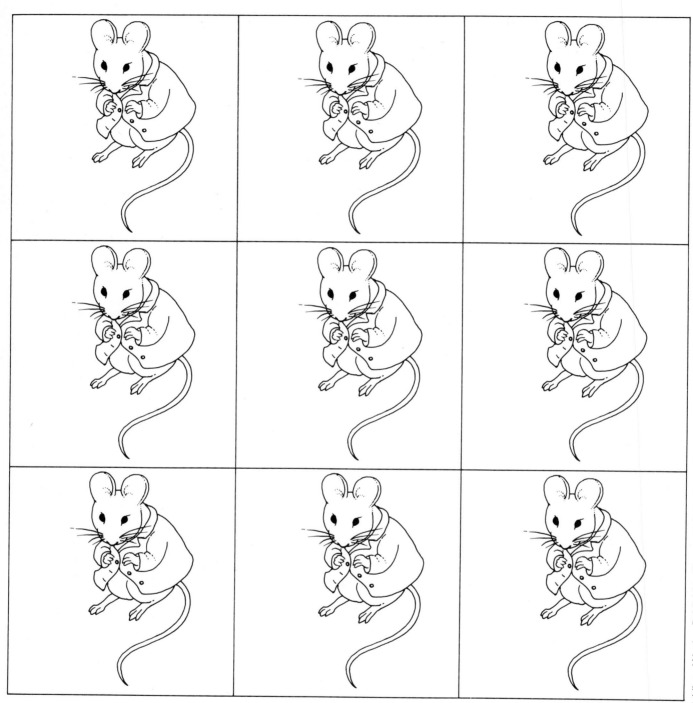

Activity 1

AREA AND PERIMETER

OVERVIEW

Activity 1 is designed to introduce students to the basic concepts of area and perimeter. However simple this activity may seem, it is essential that students understand these concepts at a concrete level. Area is typically known only as length times width, and perimeter is frequently not known at all. The concepts are conveyed through story language that parallels the mathematical language.

Students use tiles to represent small tables that form banquet tables and then find their measures. Banquet tables are always rectangular arrays, with the exception of a few odd shapes in this activity. Area is the number of small tables needed to form a banquet table. Perimeter is the number of people who can be seated at a banquet table, knowing that one small table seats four people, or one to an edge. Mathematical terms of area and perimeter are introduced after the concepts are understood in terms of tables and people. Students will adopt the mathematical language quickly or slowly, depending on their interest and level.

The story approach provides students with a means of distinguishing area from perimeter, for it is the names they confuse not the concepts. If a student asks what perimeter means, for example, responding with "people" is usually sufficient. The story interpretation does not prevent students from forming misconceptions, however. Some students will miscount the perimeter by counting border tiles instead of edges. Counting is the most prevalent means of finding measures in this activity. Rules are deliberately not introduced until the summary of Activity 2. For some students, counting will continue to be their primary strategy for measuring.

The challenge in this activity is qualitatively different from those in the succeeding activities. The purpose is to introduce new concepts and not to seek patterns and rules. Activity 4 plays a similar role for measures of solid blocks. Because this is the first time students are asked to use tiles, they may need some time to play before starting the activity. Note: If you are not using 1-inch tiles, be sure to change the scale of the figures on the worksheets for Activity 1.

Goals for students

1. Learn the story interpretations of the mathematical concepts: area is the number of small tables in a banquet table; perimeter is the number of people that can sit at a banquet table if one person sits at the outside edge of each small table.

2. Measure areas and perimeters of rectangles and other shapes formed or covered with tiles.

Materials

One-inch tiles (24 per student).

Worksheets

1-1, Rectangle Measures.

1-2, Area and Perimeter.

1-3, Extra Challenge.

1-4, Practice Exercises.

AREA AND PERIMETER

TEACHER ACTION	TEACHER TALK	EXPECTED RESPONSE
Pass out tiles. Display a single tile and place on the overhead projector.	This tile represents a small table that seats four people.	
Display two tiles together to make a banquet table.	Place two tiles together to make a banquet table. A banquet table should be in the shape of a rectangle.	▢▢
Ask.	How many people can sit at your banquet table?	Six.
Display three more tiles together to make a banquet table.	Make a banquet table with three tables.	▢▢▢
Ask.	How many people can sit at your table?	Eight.
Demonstrate counting the eight.		
Ask. Display both solutions.	Make a banquet table using four small tables. How many people can sit at your table?	Ten. ▢▢▢▢
If students offer only one arrangement, ask.	Can anyone make a different shaped table using four tiles?	⊞ Eight.
		If students object to the square, tell the students that squares are special rectangles.
	Does it seat ten people?	No.
Introduce mathematical interpretation. You may wish to introduce these ideas as questions to see whether students already know them.	The number of people that can be seated at a table is called the *perimeter*. The number of small tables needed to make a banquet table is called the *area*.	
Write the words *perimeter* and *area* on the board.		

Activity 1 *Launch*

TEACHER ACTION	TEACHER TALK	EXPECTED RESPONSE
Have students find perimeter and area of these five examples. Point to each and ask.	What is the area and the perimeter of this rectangle?	$P = 4; A = 1.$ $P = 6; A = 2.$ $P = 8; A = 3.$ $P = 10; A = 4.$ $P = 8; A = 4.$
Record the values of P and A.		
Pass out Worksheets 1-1 and 1-2.	Cover the rectangles on Worksheet 1-1 with your tiles.	
Ask.	What is the area of Figure A? What is the perimeter of Figure A?	Figure A: $A = 8, P = 12$
	Record these values.	Figure B: $A = 7, P = 16$ Figure C: $A = 9, P = 12$
Repeat for rectangles B and C.		
If there is confusion, return to story language and demonstrate.		
	Find the area and the perimeter of the figures on both pages of Worksheet 1-2.	

Activity 1 *Explore*

OBSERVATIONS

Miscounting perimeter can be the result of careless counting or counting border tiles instead of seating places.

Check answers before giving students Worksheet 1-3.

As an extra challenge, have students use Worksheet 1-3 to find different figures that will seat 20 people.

POSSIBLE RESPONSES

Ask the student to recount. If the student still counts incorrectly, go back to the single tile and count the four seating places. Then have the student demonstrate counting the seating places in a 2-by-3 figure.

Activity 1 *Summarize*

TEACHER ACTION

Review the story interpretation of area and perimeter, then ask.

Have students do Worksheet 1-4.

TEACHER TALK

What measures did you find for area and perimeter?

EXPECTED RESPONSE

Worksheet 1-2

Figure 1: $A = 12$; $P = 14$.

Figure 2: $A = 4$; $P = 10$.

Figure 3: $A = 10$; $P = 14$.

Figure 4: $A = 22$; $P = 34$.

Rectangle Measures

Figure A

Area _____

Perimeter _____

Figure B

Area _____

Perimeter _____

Figure C

Area _____

Perimeter _____

Area and Perimeter

Figure 1

Area _____

Perimeter _____

Figure 2

Area _____

Perimeter _____

Figure 3

Area _____

Perimeter _____

Worksheet 1-2

Area and Perimeter

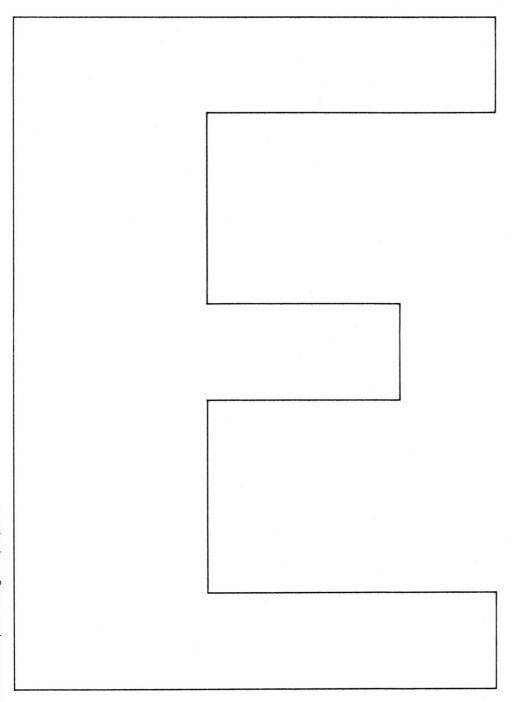

Figure 4

Area _____

Perimeter _____

NAME ____________________

Extra Challenge

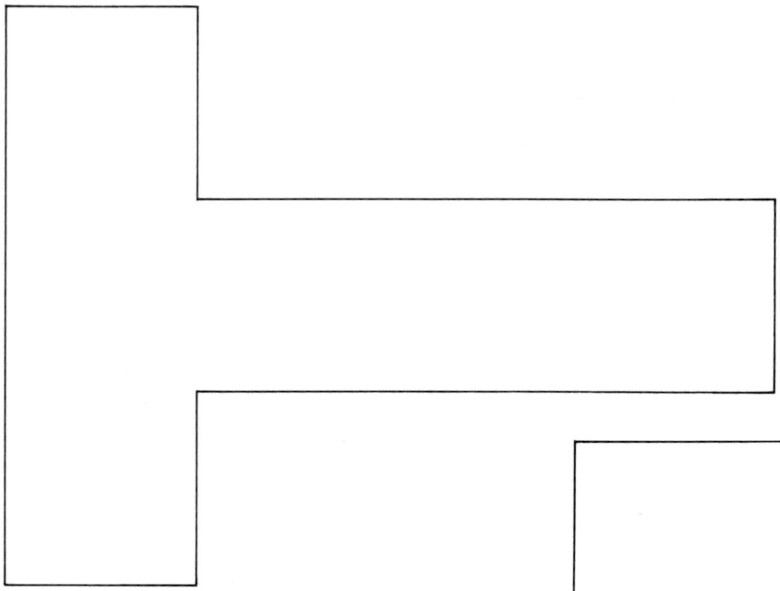

Figure 5

Area ______

Perimeter ______

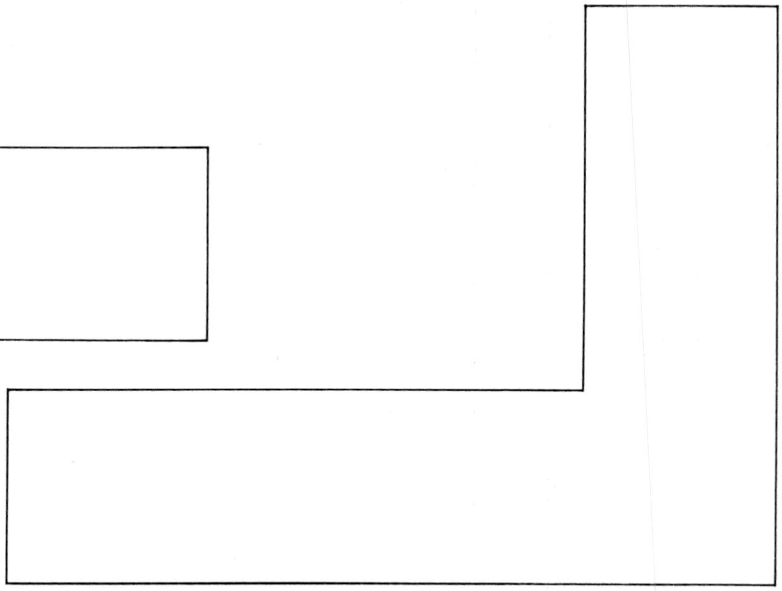

Figure 6

Area ______

Perimeter ______

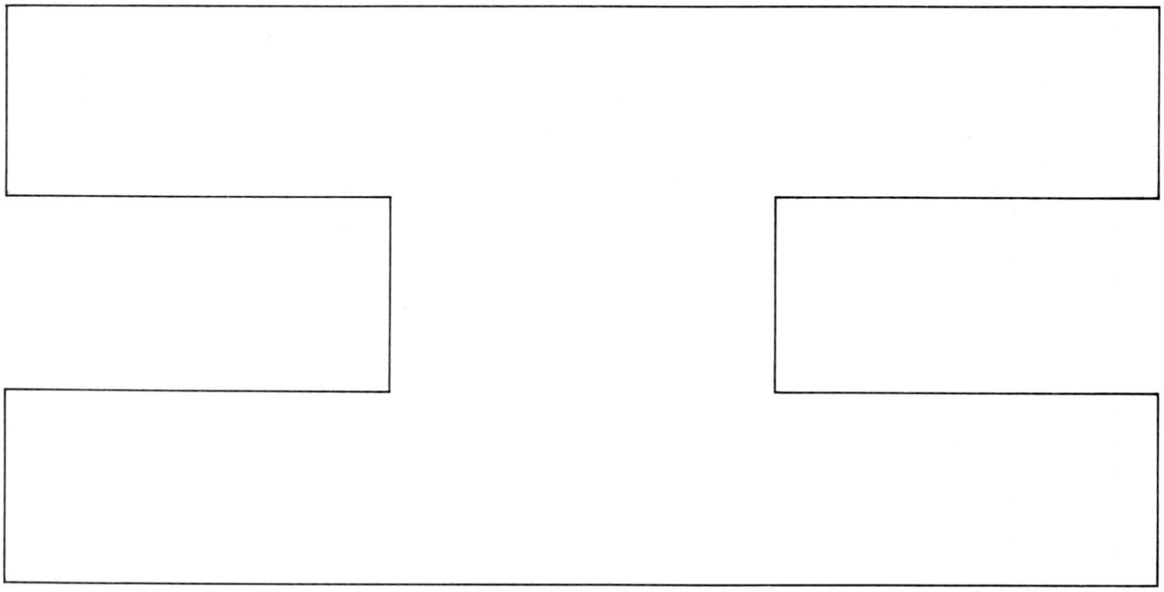

Figure 7

Area ______

Perimeter ______

Grid Paper

Practice Exercises

1. $A =$ _____ $P =$ _____

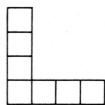

2. $A =$ _____ $P =$ _____

3. Draw in separate squares to give an area of 9, then find the perimeter.

$P =$ _____

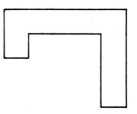

4. Draw in separate squares to give a perimeter of 18, then find the area.

$A =$ _____

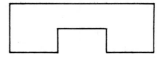

5. Add a square so that the area is 6 and the perimeter is still 12.

6. Add squares so that the perimeter is 18. What is the new area?

$A =$ _____

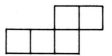

Activity 2

CONSTANT AREA—VARYING PERIMETERS

OVERVIEW

Students handle the challenge of this activity easily—finding all the different-shaped banquet tables with a specified area. The dimensions of the rectangular-shaped tables are identified by the bottom edge and side edge. This language was carefully chosen to reflect the orientation of a rectangle. The alternative language of length and width invariably leads to confusion and is, therefore, not used.

Students sometimes fail to list congruent rectangles, such as 2×12 and a 12×2, but a complete listing is helpful for recognizing and describing the relationships and rules of interest. Students readily recognize a rule for area, but a perimeter rule does not usually emerge until Activity 3. Rules are written in forms most commonly verbalized by students. For example, perimeter is written bottom edge plus side edge times 2, or $P = (B + S) \times 2$, instead of the usual $P = 2 \times (B + S)$ found in most textbooks.

Do not be surprised to find students counting to find the areas and perimeters of their rectangular banquet tables. This will persist even after the rules emerge for as long as there are concrete objects to count. Some students simply become more systematized in how they count. At this point it is easy to place too much emphasis on the rules at the expense of the students' motivation. When someone is uncertain how to find a measure, it is preferable to encourage the use of the story interpretation and counting to find the answer rather than referring to a rule. In this way, the basic concepts of area and perimeter are reinforced.

The key purpose of this activity is to have students see the impact that varying shape has on perimeter. Students will observe that for rectangles of the same area, the most elongated shape has the maximum perimeter, and the most square-like shape has the minimum perimeter. This relationship is further emphasized by having students cut rectangles out of grid paper, which can be examined when the tiled rectangles are no longer visible.

The effect of the varying dimensions for rectangles of constant area can also be viewed from a display of the paper models. The arrangement shown in the activity forms a curve, a hyperbola, that is useful for relating the graph to the concrete models and the number patterns. More graphing opportunities are presented in Activity 3.

Moving tiles around on desks or table surfaces can be noisy, so have students work on paper to dampen the sound. Construction paper is particularly effective.

Goals for students

1. Describe rectangles by dimensions: bottom edge (B) and side edge (S).
2. Measure and record dimensions, areas, and perimeters of rectangles made of tiles, using counting as the primary measuring skill.
3. Use tiles to form all rectangles of a specified area (12 or 24) and cut models from grid paper.
4. Discover and apply rules for measuring area: $A = B \times S$.
5. Discover and apply the effect of shape on rectangles with a constant area: perimeters vary; the most elongated rectangle has the largest perimeter; the most square-like rectangle has the smallest perimeter.

Activity 2

Materials

One-inch tiles (24 per student).
Two sheets of grid paper per student. (page 17)
One model of a 3 × 4 rectangle cut from grid paper.

Worksheets

*2-1, Constant Area Record Sheet.
 2-2, Extra Challenge.
 2-3, Practice Exercises.

Transparencies

Starred item should be made into a transparency.

TEACHER ACTION	TEACHER TALK	EXPECTED RESPONSE
Pass out tiles.	Make a rectangular banquet table with 12 tiles.	If incorrect responses are noted, give rapid yes/no feedback
Elicit a description of one correct example and display it.	Tell me what you built. How long is the bottom edge? How long is the side edge?	Various answers.
Ask. Review story interpretations.	What is the area? What is the perimeter?	
Ask.	Who has a different rectangle?	
Display student examples.		
Record *B*, *S*, *A*, and *P* for the two examples. Be sure to use the same recording format as Activity 2-1 uses.		

B	S	A	P
1	12	12	26
2	6	12	16
3	4	12	14
4	3	12	14
6	2	12	16
12	1	12	26

Continue asking, displaying, and recording examples until all six possibilities are found.		
Hold up a paper model of 3×4.	This is a *model* of a banquet table with a bottom edge of 3 and a side edge of 4. It helps me see what the table looks like when my tiles have been moved.	
Pass out scissors, grid paper and Worksheet 2-1.	Find all of the banquet tables that can be built with 24 small tables. Record your results on your record sheet. Cut out a model for each table.	

Activity 2 *Explore*

OBSERVATIONS	POSSIBLE RESPONSES
Some students may not use all 24 tiles.	Remind students to use all the tiles.
Some students may count the perimeter incorrectly.	Same as activity one.
Students may quit before they have found all eight rectangles.	Encourage students to find all the different rectangles.
As an extra challenge, pass out Worksheet 2-2.	

Activity 2 *Summarize*

TEACHER ACTION	TEACHER TALK	EXPECTED RESPONSE
Ask.	Who has a table with a bottom edge of one?	Record Sheet
Record on the overhead.	What is the side edge?	
Repeat for bottom edges of 2, 3, 4, 6, 8, 12, 24, *in this order*.	What is the area?	
	What is the perimeter?	
(Asking for a bottom edge of 5 and 7 can give rise to a short discussion about factors.)		

Record Sheet

B	S	A	P
1	24	24	50
2	12	24	28
3	8	24	22
4	6	24	20
6	4	24	20
8	3	24	22
12	2	24	28
24	1	24	50

TEACHER ACTION	TEACHER TALK	EXPECTED RESPONSE
	Order your rectangles from the largest perimeter to the smallest perimeter on your desks.	
Ask.	How are they changing?	From long and thin to more square-like
	Hold up the rectangle that has the largest perimeter.	
Ask.	What shape does it have?	Long and thin.
	What are its dimensions?	1×24 or 24×1
	Hold up the rectangle that has the smallest perimeter.	
Ask.	What shape does it have?	More square-like.
	What are its dimensions?	4×6 or 6×4

23

Activity 2 *Summarize*

TEACHER ACTION	TEACHER TALK	EXPECTED RESPONSE
You may want to display a prestapled model. Draw a hyperbola connecting the corners of the rectangles. Write the word *hyperbola* on the board.	Nest all eight rectangles by aligning them at their bottom left corners, beginning with the 1 × 24 and ending with the 24 × 1. The path connecting the corners of rectangles with the same area forms a curve called a hyperbola.	
Display a transparency of Worksheet 2-1 and ask. Record the patterns on the board. Verify the patterns with several examples from the table.	Look at the data on Worksheet 2-1 again. What patterns do you see?	One goes up while the other goes down; the same numbers are in reverse; the area is always 24; opposites have the same measures (3 × 8 and 8 × 3 have same perimeter and area); $B \times S = $ Area. Perimeter pattern will probably not emerge until Activity 3, but if it does, it may be described as $P = (B + S) \times 2$, or $P = (B \times 2) + (S \times 2)$.
Extend the lesson by writing dimensions and asking students to apply the rules.	Find the area (and perimeter if the rule has been given) of a rectangle 7 × 3, 5 × 8, 11 × 17, and 30 × 20.	7 × 3: $A = 21$; $P = 20$. 5 × 8: $A = 40$; $P = 26$. 11 × 17: $A = 187$; $P = 56$. 30 × 20: $A = 600$; $P = 100$.
Ask.	If you were going to make a table with 36 tiles, which table would give you the largest perimeter? Find the dimensions and perimeter.	1 × 36: $P = 74$.
Ask.	Which table would give you the smallest perimeter using 36 tiles? Find the dimensions and perimeter.	6 × 6: $P = 24$.
Assign Worksheet 2-3.		

Constant Area Record Sheet

Dimensions		Area	Perimeter
Bottom Edge	Side Edge	Number of Tables	Number of People

Extra Challenge

1. If you had 100 small tables to make into a banquet table, what is the greatest number of people you could seat at the banquet table?

   Greatest _____ with $B =$ _____ and $S =$ _____

   What is the fewest number of people you could seat at the banquet table?

   Fewest _____ with $B =$ _____ and $S =$ _____

2. What if you had 200 small tables to make into a banquet table?

   Greatest _____ with $B =$ _____ and $S =$ _____

   Fewest _____ with $B =$ _____ and $S =$ _____

3. If you had 90 small tables, what arrangement would seat the fewest number of people at the banquet table?

   Fewest _____ with $B =$ _____ and $S =$ _____

   What arrangement would seat the greatest number of people at the banquet table?

   Greatest _____ with $B =$ _____ and $S =$ _____

4. If you had 1,144 small tables, what arrangement would seat the greatest number of people?

   Greatest: Arrangement _____   People _____

   What arrangement would seat the fewest number of people?

   Fewest: Arrangement _____   People _____

Worksheet 2-2

Practice Exercises

You will need a sheet of grid paper.

1. On the grid paper, draw *all* possible banquet tables that can be made in the shape of a rectangle using 18 small tables (tiles). Give the area and perimeter of each banquet table.

2. a) Of the banquet tables you found in problem 1, which table will seat the greatest number of people? What are its dimensions?

$B =$ _____ $S =$ _____ $P =$ _____

b) Which of the tables from problem 1 will seat the fewest number of people?

$B =$ _____ $S =$ _____ $P =$ _____

3. a) Use the same procedure as in problem 1 but with 72 small tables. Which rectangle would have the greatest perimeter?

$B =$ _____ $S =$ _____ $P =$ _____

b) Which rectangle would have the smallest perimeter?

$B =$ _____ $S =$ _____ $P =$ _____

Activity 3

CONSTANT PERIMETER—VARYING AREAS

OVERVIEW

Holding the perimeter constant and allowing the area to vary is significantly more difficult for students than the reverse task. In earlier activities, students needed only to rearrange a fixed number of tiles; in this activity, tiles are added on and taken off until a rectangle with the correct perimeter has been found. In order to form all possible banquet tables that seat 24 people, students will need to pool their tiles or be issued extra tiles because the largest table contains 36 tiles.

By this time all students are aware of the area rule even if they actually count the number of tiles. Unless it was offered in the previous activity, the perimeter rule should emerge as you summarize. Suggest that students look at the sum of the bottom and side edges if a hint is needed.

Again, paper models cut from grid paper help students recognize that for rectangles of the same perimeter, the smallest area occurs with the most elongated rectangle, and the greatest area occurs with the most square-like rectangle. When the models are arranged to show the effect of the changing dimensions, a straight line appears. For students able to plot points, there is an additional graphing exercise that uses data from Activities 2 and 3 and produces two different looking curves, including a parabola.

Goals for students

1. Measure dimensions, areas, and perimeters of rectangles made of tiles by counting or applying rules.
2. Use tiles to form all rectangles of a specified perimeter (12 or 24) and cut models from grid paper.
3. Discover and apply rules for measuring area and perimeter: $A = B \times S$; $P = (B + S) \times 2$ or $(B \times 2) + (S \times 2)$.
4. Discover and apply the effect of shape on rectangles with a constant perimeter: areas vary; the most elongated rectangle has the smallest area; and the most square-like rectangle has the largest area.

Materials

One-inch tiles (24 per student).

One sheet of grid paper per student.

One set of rectangles with perimeter 24 cut, arranged, and stapled for demonstration.

Worksheets

*3-1, Constant Perimeter Record Sheet.

3-2, Extra Challenge.

3-3, Practice Exercises.

3-4, Fixed Perimeter Graph (Optional).

3-5, Fixed Area Graph.

Transparencies

Starred item should be made into a transparency.

CONSTANT PERIMETER—VARYING AREAS

TEACHER ACTION	TEACHER TALK	EXPECTED RESPONSE
Pass out tiles. Give rapid yes/no feedback.	Build a banquet table that will seat 12 people.	Five possibilities:
Elicit a description of one correct example and display it.	Tell me what you built. How long is the bottom edge? How long is the side edge?	1 × 5 5 × 1 2 × 4 4 × 2 3 × 3
Ask. Review the story interpretation.	What is the area?	
	What is the perimeter?	
Record B, S, P, and A.		

B	S	P	A
1	5	12	5
2	4	12	8
3	3	12	9
4	2	12	8
5	1	12	5

TEACHER ACTION	TEACHER TALK
Continue asking, displaying, and recording measures until all five examples are found. Order will depend on student response.	Who has another example?
Pass out scissors, grid paper and Worksheet 3-1.	Find all of the banquet tables that can be built that will seat 24 people. Cut out a model for each and record the results.

OBSERVATIONS

Holding the perimeter constant is a more difficult cognitive task than holding the area constant. With the number of tiles no longer held constant, the students need to add or remove individual tiles to find rectangles with a fixed perimeter.

As an extra challenge, pass out Worksheet 3-2.

POSSIBLE RESPONSES

Be prepared for some students to be frustrated in trying to find examples. There will be a lot of miscounting. Encourage students to try adding on or taking off more tiles so as to maintain a rectangle or to try changing only one dimension at a time.

Activity 3 *Summarize*

TEACHER ACTION	TEACHER TALK	EXPECTED RESPONSE

TEACHER ACTION

Ask.
Record on the overhead.

Repeat for bottom edges of 2 through 11.

Ask.
Record the patterns on the chalkboard.
Verify the patterns with several examples from the table.

Extend the lesson by asking students to apply rules.

TEACHER TALK

Who has a model with a bottom edge of 1?

What is the side edge?

What is the perimeter?

What is the area?

What patterns do you see?

Find the area and perimeter of a rectangle 4 × 21.

What is the area and perimeter of a rectangle 17 × 3

What is the area and perimeter of a rectangle 10 × 30?

EXPECTED RESPONSE

B	S	P	A
1	11	24	11
2	10	24	20
3	9	24	27
4	8	24	32
5	7	24	35
6	6	24	36
7	5	24	35
8	4	24	32
9	3	24	27
10	2	24	20
11	1	24	11

Numbers are reversed; numbers are consecutive from 1 to 11 and 11 to 1; $B \times S = $ Area; $B + S = 12$; $P = (B + S) \times 2$; $P = (B \times 2) + (S \times 2)$.

$A = 84$; $P = 50$.

$A = 51$; $P = 40$.

$A = 300$; $P = 80$.

Activity 3 *Summarize*

TEACHER ACTION	TEACHER TALK	EXPECTED RESPONSE
Ask.	Take the models of your rectangles and order them from smallest area to largest area on your desks.	
	How are they changing?	Tall and thin to square.
Ask.	Hold up the rectangle that has the smallest area. What shape does it have? What are its dimensions?	Long and thin; 1×11 or 11×1.
Ask.	Hold up the rectangle that has the largest area. What shape does it have? What are its dimensions?	Square; 6×6.
Assign Worksheet 3-3.		
Display a prestapled model of aligned rectangles.	Nest all eleven rectangles by aligning them at the bottom left corners, beginning with the 1×11 and ending with the 11×1.	
Pass out Worksheet 3-4.		

MATHEMATICS DEPARTMENT
ALVERNO COLLEGE
MILWAUKEE, WI 53234-3922

Activity 3 *Summarize*

TEACHER ACTION	TEACHER TALK	EXPECTED RESPONSE
Ask and draw the curve.	Is the curve for rectangles with constant perimeters the same shape as the one for rectangles with constant area? How do they compare?	No; this one is a straight line, the other was a curved line (a hyperbola).
	Graph the ordered pairs of bottom edge against the area for rectangles of constant perimeter.	
Ask, tell, and write the word *parabola* on the board.	What shape is this curve? It is called a *parabola*.	
Pass out Worksheet 3-5. Display data from Worksheet 2-1.	If you graph the bottom edge against the perimeter for rectangles of constant area using the data from Worksheet 2-1, you will get another curve variation.	
Ask.	If you were going to form a rectangle of tiles with a perimeter of 36, which dimensions would give you the smallest area?	1×17; $A = 17$.
Ask.	Which dimensions would give you the largest area?	9×9; $A = 81$.

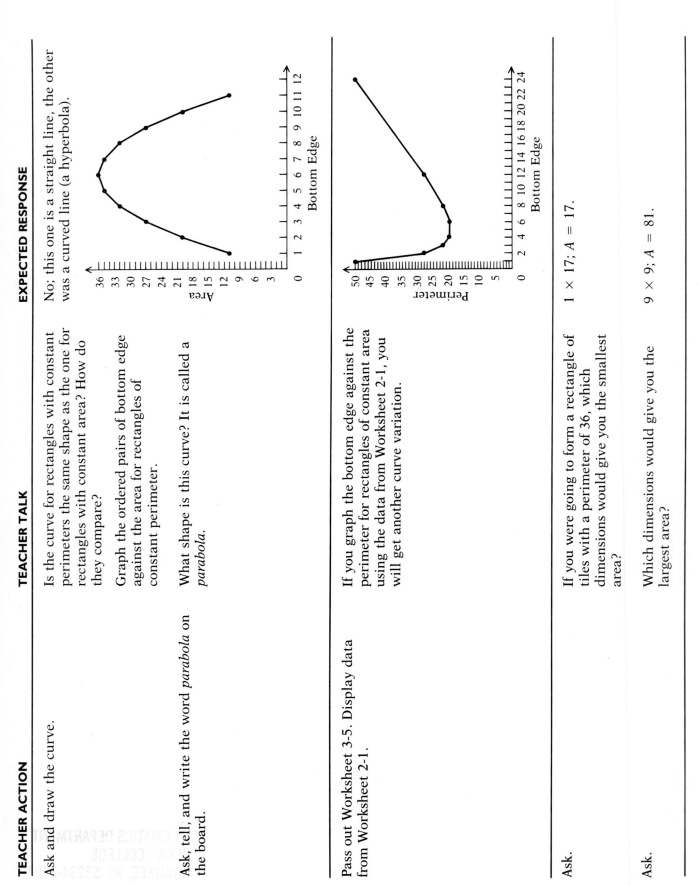

Constant Perimeter Record Sheet

Dimensions		Perimeter	Area
B	*S*		

Extra Challenge

1. a) What is the greatest number of tables needed to seat 100 people?

b) What is the fewest number of tables needed to seat 100 people?

2. a) What is the greatest number of tables needed to seat 250 people?

b) What is the fewest number of tables needed to seat 250 people?

Practice Exercises

You will need a sheet of grid paper.

1. On grid paper, draw all the possible banquet tables in the shape of a rectangle that will seat 18 people. Write down the area and perimeter of each banquet table:

2. Using the rectangles you found in problem 1, answer the following questions.

   a) What is the fewest number of tables you need?

   $A = $ _____ with dimensions $B = $ _____ , $S = $ _____

   b) What is the greatest number of tables you need?

   $A = $ _____ with dimensions $B = $ _____ , $S = $ _____

3. a) For a rectangle with perimeter of 72, what rectangle has the largest area?

   $A = $ _____ with dimensions $B = $ _____ , $S = $ _____

   b) What rectangle has the smallest area?

   $A = $ _____ with dimensions $B = $ _____ , $S = $ _____

Fixed Perimeter Graph

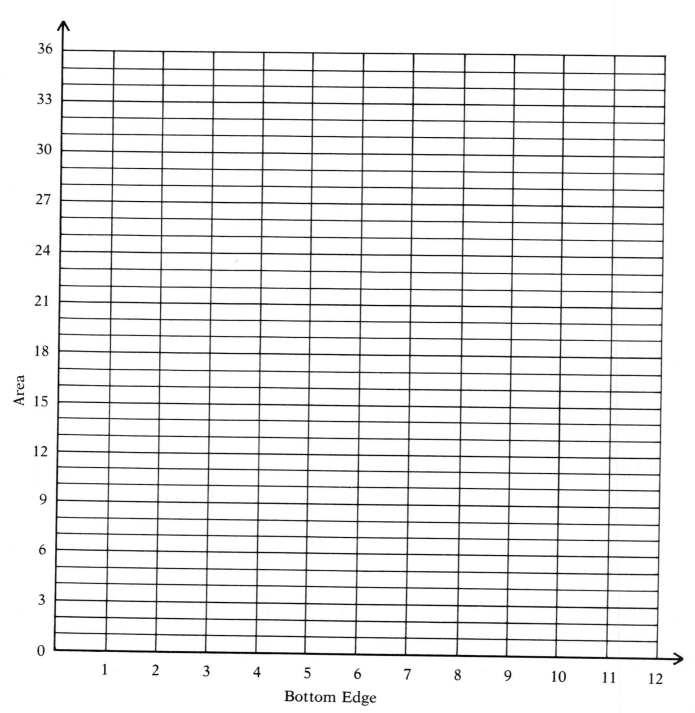

Worksheet 3-4

Fixed Area Graph

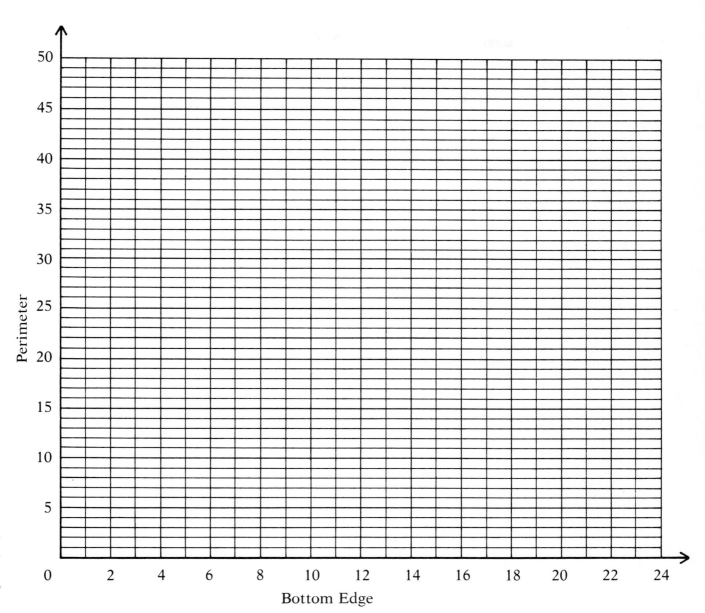

Perimeter

Bottom Edge

Activity 4

SPACE FOOD PACKAGES

OVERVIEW

Activity 4 introduces more new concepts—volume and surface area. The story involves the packaging of food for travel in space. A cube represents one day's food supply, which means that volume is interpreted as the number of days the food supply will last. Special paper known as a space armor jacket is used to wrap each package. By counting the number of squares in a space armor jacket, each worth $1, the space armor cost, or surface area, is determined.

The students are working with colored blocks and may need some time to become familiar with them. Each student should be given cubes of only one color so they do not need to spend time trading colors with their neighbors.

Students begin the activity by trying to wrap a single cube in a square paper without having any overlaps or holes. Their behaviors are most enjoyable to observe because this task is highly dependent on some special abilities, and a variety of skill levels become obvious very quickly. Some students easily cut a jacket on their first attempt while others are frustrated by trying to wrap the cube like a present and not knowing what to do with the overlap. Many students become intrigued with the challenge of finding as many different-shaped jackets as possible for one cube. Once someone realizes the individual squares can be subdivided, however, it becomes apparent there are infinite jacket patterns rather than the eleven shown here.

Another surprise comes when students are asked to package a specified number of cubes and wrap them in a jacket cut from an existing pattern. Some students have trouble arranging the cubes to make this possible. Cutting jackets for the different-sized packages is so appealing for some students that they forget the directions and cut more than one jacket pattern per package. Some students may begin thinking about the cost efficiency of a package, which will be addressed explicitly in Activity 6.

At the end of this activity, students are asked how many jackets for a one-day supply of food can be made from jackets for more than one-day's supply of food. The concept will be elaborated upon in Activity 8 to aid students in solving the Mouse and Elephant questions.

It is appropriate to review the Mouse and Elephant questions either before or after Activity 4 so that students may revise their original predictions.

Goals for students

1. Learn the story interpretations of the mathematical concepts: volume is the number of food pellets (cubes) in a package, or the number of days the food supply will last—each cube is a one day supply; surface area is the number of squares used to cover the solid block, or the cost of a space armor jacket if each square is $1.

2. Find different patterns of space armor jackets for a cube.

3. Cut one piece space armor jackets to exactly fit food packages.

4. Measure the cost of a space armor jacket if each square is $1.

5. Fill space armor jackets with cubes and measure the number of days the food supply will last by counting the cubes.

6. Describe solid blocks by dimensions: bottom front edge (BF), bottom side edge (BS), and height (H).

Activity 4

Copyright © 1986 Addison-Wesley Publishing Company, Inc.

Materials

2-cm cubes (24 per student, in plastic bags).
Three sheets of grid paper per student (Materials 4-1).

Worksheets

*4-1, Space Food Packages Record Sheet.
 4-2, Space Armor Jackets.
 4-3, Extra Challenge.
 4-4, Practice Exercises.

Transparencies

Starred item should be made into a transparency.

Activity 4 *Launch*   **SPACE FOOD PACKAGES**

TEACHER ACTION	TEACHER TALK	EXPECTED RESPONSE
Pass out cubes, scissors, and 2 or 3 sheets of grid paper (Materials 4-1). Display 2-cm cubes and tell the story.	For space travel one day's supply of food is concentrated in this cube, which we call a food pellet. To prevent the food from contamination during the flight we must wrap it in very special paper called space armor.	
Display space armor jacket paper—square paper—and direct.	Cut a jacket of space armor that covers this cube exactly. There can be no overlap and no holes! The space armor jacket must be in one piece! Edges of squares must connect, not just points.	
		Point out overlaps, nonconnected edges, and incomplete jackets.
		For students who have serious difficulty cutting a jacket for the cube, try placing the cube on one square and then rolling it while drawing the pattern for them to cut.
When a student finds one jacket, ask.	Can you cut different-shaped space armor jackets?	
As several jacket patterns emerge, hold them up.	These are some of the jackets I have seen.	More variations will emerge.

43

Activity 4 *Launch*

TEACHER ACTION	TEACHER TALK	EXPECTED RESPONSE
Display jacket variations as they emerge. (These can be taped to the chalkboard or pinned on the bulletin board.)	Who has a different-shaped jacket?	It is not necessary that every student have all eleven variations shown. Allow enough time for everyone to have several variations. Some students will realize that a square can be split, which leads to many more variations (◁).
Encourage students to find yet another variation. Continue at least until all eleven of the variations are displayed.		

a b c d e f g h i j k

TEACHER ACTION	TEACHER TALK	EXPECTED RESPONSE
When all the variations have been displayed, tell the story.	Each jacket is made up of space armor, which costs $1 per square.	
Ask.	What is the cost of wrapping one food pellet in space armor?	$6.00.
Pass out Worksheet 4-1. Record.	Label your jacket A for package A and record its cost on your record sheet Worksheet 4-1.	

Package	Number of Days	Cost
A	1	$6

TEACHER ACTION	TEACHER TALK	EXPECTED RESPONSE
Ask.	Do different jackets have different costs?	No; each one costs $6.00.

Activity 4 *Launch*

TEACHER ACTION	TEACHER TALK	EXPECTED RESPONSE

Display a two-cube package.

Now make one package for a two-day food supply and cut one space armor jacket that will cover both cubes.

Some of the same difficulties can be anticipated. While lots of variations are possible, only one jacket is needed.

Example:

As an extra challenge have students who finish early cut a different-shaped jacket.

Ask.

What is the space armor cost for wrapping two food pellets?

$10. If students have different answers, ask them to check to see if the jacket really covers properly.

Record.

Label your jacket B and record the number of day's food supply it is and the cost of the space armor.

Package	Number of Days	Cost
A	1	$6
B	2	$10
C	3	$14

Display a three-cube package and have students determine the space armor jacket cost; have them record their data as before.

45

TEACHER ACTION	TEACHER TALK	EXPECTED RESPONSE
	This time, package a four-day supply of food pellets and cut a space armor jacket.	
Ask.	What is the cost of this space armor jacket?	Both $18 and $16 are correct, although $18 may be the only one given at this point.
Ask. (Do this whether one or both answers were given because you want students to have both jackets.)	Can you arrange your cubes differently?	Yes. If students have cut a $1 \times 4 \times 1$ jacket they will show $2 \times 2 \times 1$, or vice versa.
Ask. Both answers should be known to all students.	Cut out a space armor jacket for the new one.	
	What is the cost of this jacket?	$18; $16.
Ask.	How can we describe our two packages so that we know which one is which?	Give dimensions.
Ask.	Place your long package of four cubes in front of you so that it is one cube along the bottom front edge, four along the bottom side edge, and one high. Do you all have the same package placed in front of you in the same way?	
Ask.	Label the jacket for this package D. On your recording sheet label the last three columns BF for *bottom front edge*, BS for *bottom side edge*, H for *height*, and record all the information.	Yes. (If not, some changing will occur.)

	BF	BS	H
·	·	·	·
·	·	·	·
D	4	18	1

Activity 4 *Launch*

TEACHER ACTION	TEACHER TALK	EXPECTED RESPONSE
Ask and record.	What did you record?	

			BF	BS	H
·	·	·	·	·	·
D	4	18	1	4	1

TEACHER ACTION	TEACHER TALK
Ask.	Label the jacket for the other package E and record the number of day's food supply and cost of the space armor.
Ask.	How might the four cubes be arranged in package E, which costs $16?

Package	Number of Days	Cost	BF	BS	H
·	·	·	·	·	·
E	4	16	2	2	1
			or 2	1	2
			or 1	2	2

(Solicit all three arrangements.)

TEACHER ACTION	TEACHER TALK	EXPECTED RESPONSE
	We are more interested in different costs that in different ways to orient your packages, so we will not record variations in dimensions anymore unless the space armor costs are different.	
	Look at your package and write down the dimensions that fit your arrangement of package E.	
Ask and record.	What are the dimensions of package A? What are the dimensions of package B? What are the dimensions of package C?	$1 \times 1 \times 1$ $1 \times 2 \times 1$ } or one of the variations. $1 \times 3 \times 1$
	Record these on your worksheets.	

TEACHER ACTION	TEACHER TALK	EXPECTED RESPONSE
Pass out Worksheet 4-2.		
Ask.	These are space armor jackets that cost $1 per square. How much does the eight-day package cost? How much does the six-day package cost?	Eight-day: $24. Six-day: $26.
	Cut these two space armor jackets out and fill them with space food. Each cube is one day's supply of food.	Some students will have trouble arranging the cubes so that the jackets fit. Encourage them to arrange their cubes in another way as needed.
Ask.	How many cubes did you put in the $26 package? Label this jacket F.	6
Repeat.	How many cubes did you put in the $24 package? Label this package H. Record the information about packages F and H on your worksheet.	8
Ask.	Which package is more economical? Why?	The eight-day jacket; it costs less than the six-day jacket.
	Find all the other ways to package your six- and eight-day food supplies and cut a space armor jacket for each arrangement that gives you a different cost. Label your jackets with the remaining letters and record all the measures.	

Activity 4 *Explore*

OBSERVATIONS	POSSIBLE RESPONSES
Students may have trouble stacking the cubes to obtain all the different arrangements.	Ask if they have found packages for all the letters through J.
Cutting a pattern may continue to be a problem for some students.	Select one of the jackets with a simple design and suggest students try to make the new one as much like it as possible. This jacket is easily adapted for varied sizes.
As an extra challenge, suggest that students cut jackets for blocks shown on Worksheet 4-3.	

Activity 4 *Summarize*

TEACHER ACTION	TEACHER TALK	EXPECTED RESPONSE
Ask.	For package A, the single cube, we found many different patterns for the space armor jacket. Did the different shaped jackets have different costs?	No; all cost the same.
	Why?	The cube did not change only the arrangement of squares needed to cover the cube.
Ask.	How did we find the cost of a jacket?	Count the number of squares.
Define and ask.	The number of squares needed to completely cover a solid block of cubes is the *surface area*. What is the *surface area* of A?	6
	The number of cubes, or day's food supply in a package, is the *volume*. What is the *volume* of A?	1
Ask.	What is the surface area of B? What is the volume of B?	

	Surface Area	Volume
B:	10	2
C:	14	3
D:	18	4
E:	16	4
F:	26	6
H:	24	8

Repeat the questions for C, D, E, F, H.

50

Activity 4 *Summarize*

TEACHER ACTION	TEACHER TALK	EXPECTED RESPONSE
Ask and record.	What other packages did you find with a volume of 6? Give the surface area and dimensions. What other packages did you find with a volume of 8?	Complete table
	Give the surface area and dimensions.	
Ask.	For different packages with the same number of cubes, was the cost of the space armor jacket always the same?	No, shape makes a difference.
	How do we describe a package so someone else can build it?	Dimensions *BF, BS, H*.
	What do the jackets have to do with the Mouse and Elephant question?	Space armor jackets are like mouse coats.
	What is the surface area of the smallest package, A, with only one cube? What is the surface area of package D?	A = 6 D = 18
	Consider only the actual number of squares in each jacket. How many A-sized jackets could be made from a D-sized jacket? Why?	Three; because D has a surface area of 18 and A has a surface area of 6. There are three A sizes in D.
	How many A-sized jackets could be made from an H-sized jacket? Why?	Four; because H has a surface area of 24 and there are four A sizes in D.

Complete table:

F	6	26	1	6	1
G	6	22	2	3	1
H	8	24	2	2	2
I	8	28	2	4	1
J	8	34	1	8	1

Activity 4 *Summarize*

TEACHER ACTION	TEACHER TALK	EXPECTED RESPONSE
This is a good time to review the Mouse and Elephant questions with the class.		
Ask.	Do you remember the Mouse and Elephant questions we want to answer by the end of the unit?	
	How many mice are needed on the scales to balance the elephant?	
	How many mouse coats are needed to sew a coat for the elephant?	
	You might want to reconsider your earlier guesses and change your answers to these questions.	
Assign Worksheet 4-4.		

Grid Paper

Space Food Packages
Record Sheet

Space food package	Number of days the food supply will last	Cost of space armor jacket			
A					
B					
C					
D					
E					
F					
G					
H					
I					
J					

Worksheet 4-1

NAME _____

Space Armor Jackets

Cut out the patterns of the space armor jackets and find the cost of wrapping the eight-day and six-day supplies of food pellets.

8-Day Package

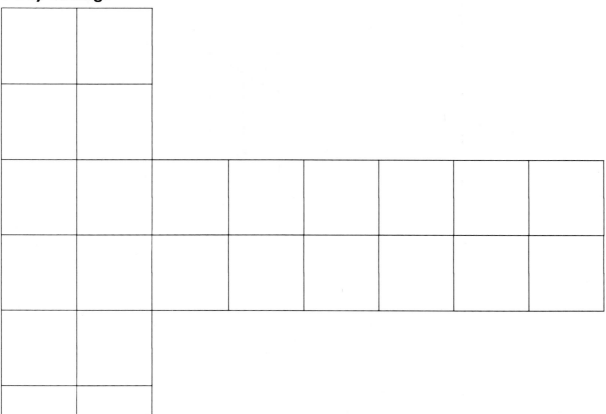

6-Day Package

Extra Challenge

Cut jackets for the food packages illustrated below and find the cost for each:

1. L-shape

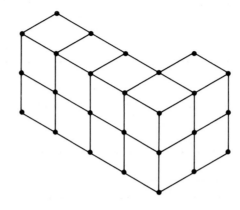

2. Half-cube

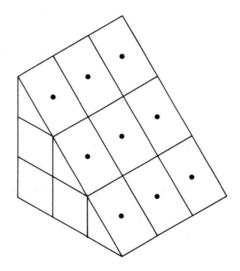

3. Square doughnut

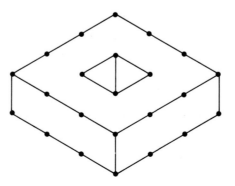

Practice Exercises

Find the number of days the food supply will last, or the volume of each space armor jacket. Also, find the surface area (the cost of the jacket) and the dimensions of the package.

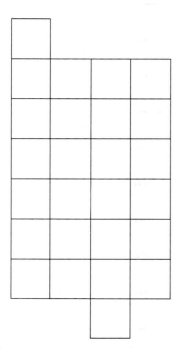

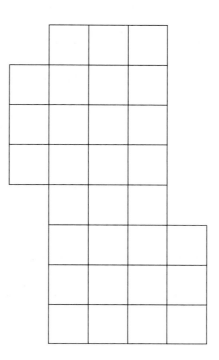

Volume = _____   Surface Area = _____   Volume = _____   Surface Area = _____

Dimensions = _____ , _____ , _____   Dimensions = _____ , _____ , _____

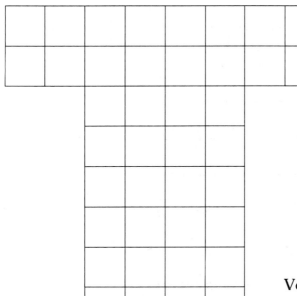

Volume = _____   Surface Area = _____

Dimensions = _____ , _____ , _____

Practice Exercises

Some of these space armor jackets cover one cube, some do not.
Circle the numbers of the jackets that *do* cover one cube.

1.
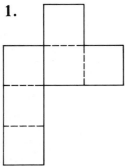

2.
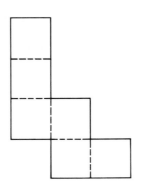

3.
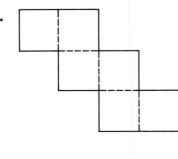

4.
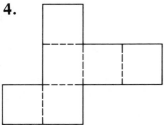

5.

6.
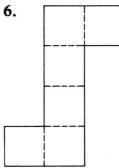

7.
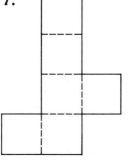

8.
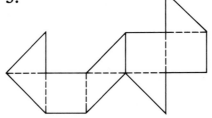

9.
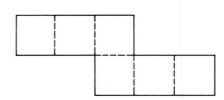

10.
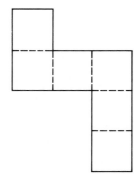

11.
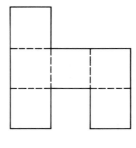

12.
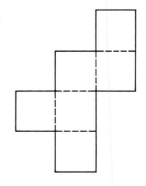

Worksheet 4-4, page 2

CONSTANT VOLUME—VARYING SURFACE AREA

OVERVIEW

In Activity 5, volume is held constant while students look for variations in shape and surface area. Instead of the mathematical relatedness of area and surface area, students tend to think of area and volume as being similar because both measures are obtained by counting objects. Similarly, they tend to link perimeter and surface area because both measure around an object. For students, the task of varying shape while holding volume constant is similar to that of holding area constant.

At this stage many students count cubes and squares one-by-one rather than seeking a more organized procedure to measure volume and surface area. Errors are easily made when counting the surface area, because the bottom face is often forgotten.

As with rectangles, dimensions of a solid block are labeled with language reflecting its orientation—the bottom front edge, the bottom side edge, and the height. Unlike earlier activities, only packages with different costs need to be listed in Activity 5. Because as many as six different orientations can be found for a solid block, it needs to be made clear that recording only one is sufficient. This is not immediately obvious to the students.

The volume rule is easily elicited during the summary, but the rule for surface area is not. From their block models and their data, students discover that when volume is held constant, the maximum surface area occurs with the most elongated package and the minimum surface area occurs with the most cube-like package.

Activities 5 and 6 provide a good opportunity for students who have been studying factors to make use of their understanding to analyze the possible space food packages.

Goals for students

1. Measure and record dimensions, volume, and surface area of rectangular solid blocks made of cubes, using counting as the primary measuring skill.

2. Use cubes to form solid blocks with specific volume (12 or 24) but with different surface areas.

3. Discover and apply rules for measuring volume:
   $V = BF \times BS \times H$.

4. Discover and apply the effect of holding volume constant while varying the dimensions of solid blocks: surface area changes; the most compact or cube-like shape has the minimum surface area; the most elongated shape has the maximum surface area.

5. Build a solid block with surface area constraints.

Materials

2-cm cubes (24 per student).

Worksheets

5-1, Solid Blocks.
*5-2, Constant Volume Record Sheet.
5-3, Extra Challenge.
5-4, Practice Exercises.

Transparencies

Starred item should be made into a transparency.

CONSTANT VOLUME—VARYING SURFACE AREA

TEACHER ACTION	TEACHER TALK	EXPECTED RESPONSE
Pass out cubes.	Build a solid block with bottom front edge of 3, bottom side edge of 2, and height of 1.	
Ask.	How many day's food supply are in this package?	6
	Can we find the cost of the space armor without cutting a jacket? How?	Yes; count squares on top and bottom, left and right, and back and front faces, or count the number of squares on opposite faces.
	What is the cost of the space armor jacket for this package?	$22
	Why?	$6 + 6 = 12$ or $(6 + 2 + 3) \times 2 = 22.$ $2 + 2 = 4$ $\underline{3 + 3 = 6}$ 22
		Students often forget to count the bottom face and may answer 16.
Ask.	Can you make a different-shaped package for six-day supply of food? What are its dimensions?	Yes.
		$1 \times 6 \times 1$, or variation.
Review and ask.	Remember, the space armor cost is the same as the surface area. What is the surface area of this block?	$(4 \times 6) + 2 = 26$ Four faces of six squares and two ends of 1 each.
	Remember, the volume is the number of day's food supply the package holds. What is the volume of this package?	6

Activity 5 *Launch*

TEACHER ACTION	TEACHER TALK	EXPECTED RESPONSE
Pass out Worksheet 5-1.	Stack 12 cubes on rectangle A so that they fill the rectangle.	If students' responses are incorrect, give yes/no feedback.
Define.	We always stack space food in rectangular solids, which we call solid blocks.	
Ask.	What is the bottom front edge? What is the bottom side edge? What is the height? What is the volume? What is the surface area? Record your answers.	Some students may still forget to count the bottom face for the surface area.

<table>
<tr><td colspan="4">Dimensions</td><td></td><td></td></tr>
<tr><td></td><td>BF</td><td>BS</td><td>H</td><td>Vol.</td><td>S.A.</td></tr>
<tr><td>A</td><td>3</td><td>2</td><td>2</td><td>12</td><td>32</td></tr>
<tr><td>B</td><td>1</td><td>4</td><td>3</td><td>12</td><td>38</td></tr>
<tr><td>C</td><td>2</td><td>1</td><td>6</td><td>12</td><td>40</td></tr>
</table>

TEACHER ACTION	TEACHER TALK	EXPECTED RESPONSE
Repeat the questions for rectangles B and C.		
Ask.	Are there other ways 12 cubes can be arranged to give a different surface area?	Yes.
	Give the measures.	

<table>
<tr><td colspan="3">Dimensions</td><td></td><td></td></tr>
<tr><td>BF</td><td>BS</td><td>H</td><td>Vol.</td><td>S.A.</td></tr>
<tr><td>1</td><td>12</td><td>1</td><td>12</td><td>50</td></tr>
</table>

		If students simply suggest alternative orientations ($3 \times 2 \times 2$ as opposed to $2 \times 3 \times 2$), remind them that we are only interested in variations that give different surface areas.
Pass out Worksheet 5-2.	Find all the ways to package 24 day's supply of food to give different costs for the space armor jackets.	
	Record the dimensions, volume, and surface area of each on Worksheet 5-2.	

Activity 5 *Explore*

OBSERVATIONS

Many students have difficulty counting the surface area correctly.

Students will be unsure whether they should write down a solid block twice if it has a different orientation. When working with rectangles, we considered 3 × 4 different from 4 × 3. In this situation we are primarily interested in finding packages with different space armor jacket costs.

The students may not find all the possibilities.

As an extra challenge, pass out Worksheet 5-3.

POSSIBLE RESPONSES

Help the students see that opposite sides have the same measure, so they can count them pair-wise.

Check to see whether students know that the same block with a different orientation will cost the same amount. Encourage them to look for different blocks with new costs.

There are six different possibilities.

TEACHER ACTION	TEACHER TALK	EXPECTED RESPONSE
Ask and record.	Who has one example of how to package 24 days of food? What are the dimensions (*BF*, *BS*, *H*)? What is the volume? What is the surface area?	<table><tr><td colspan="3">Dimensions</td><td rowspan="2">Vol.</td><td rowspan="2">S.A.</td></tr><tr><td>*BF*</td><td>*BS*</td><td>*H*</td></tr><tr><td>1</td><td>1</td><td>24</td><td>24</td><td>98</td></tr><tr><td>1</td><td>2</td><td>12</td><td>24</td><td>76</td></tr><tr><td>1</td><td>3</td><td>8</td><td>24</td><td>70</td></tr><tr><td>1</td><td>4</td><td>6</td><td>24</td><td>68</td></tr><tr><td>2</td><td>2</td><td>6</td><td>24</td><td>56</td></tr><tr><td>2</td><td>3</td><td>4</td><td>24</td><td>52</td></tr></table>
Continue to gather data until all six different costs appear. Order of recording will depend on students' responses.	Who has a different example?	
Ask.	Can packages with the same volume have different surface areas? Why?	Yes, by making different shapes with different dimensions—not just turning the package to reorder the dimensions.
Ask.	Which solid package of 24 cubes has the maximum surface area?	$1 \times 1 \times 24$; S.A. = 98.
	Which one has the minimum surface area?	$2 \times 3 \times 4$; S.A. = 52.
	Describe the shapes of volume 24 that have maximum and minimum surface areas.	The most elongated shape has the maximum surface area and the most cube-like shape has the minimum surface area.

Activity 5 *Summarize*

TEACHER ACTION	TEACHER TALK	EXPECTED RESPONSE
Ask.	Do you see a pattern for finding volume?	
Record the pattern on the board.		
Verify the pattern with several examples from the table.		$V = BF \times BS \times H.$
Ask.	Do you see a pattern for finding surface area?	A pattern for finding surface area *rarely* emerges, but students may see that opposite faces are the same and are rectangles.
Extend the idea by asking students to apply rules.	Suppose you had a rectangle measuring $1 \times 7 \times 3$. What is the volume?	$V = 21$; S.A. $= 62$.
Repeat for surface area if some usable rule emerges.	What is the volume of a rectangle measuring $2 \times 5 \times 4$? $11 \times 6 \times 3$? $30 \times 40 \times 25$?	$V = 40$; S.A. $= 76$. $V = 198$; S.A. $= 234$. $V = 30,000$; S.A. $= 5,900$.
Ask.	What is the most expensive way to package 36 cubes? What are the dimensions and cost?	$1 \times 1 \times 36$ at \$146.
	What is the least expensive way to package 36 cubes? What are the dimensions and cost?	$3 \times 3 \times 4$ at \$66.
You may want to repeat the questions with 120 cubes; this activity would provide an opportunity to examine use of factors more carefully.		Most expensive $1 \times 1 \times 120$ at \$482. Least expensive $4 \times 5 \times 6$ at \$148.

NAME _____

Solid Blocks

Place 12 cubes on each rectangle.

Rectangle A

Height _____

Bottom side

edge _____

Bottom front edge _____

Rectangle B

Height _____

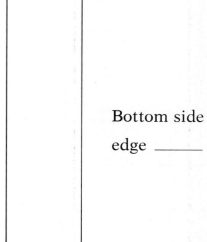

Bottom side

edge _____

Bottom front edge _____

Rectangle C

Height _____

Bottom side edge _____

Bottom front edge _____

Constant Volume Record Sheet

Dimensions			Volume	Surface Area
BF	BS	H		

Extra Challenge

1. A team of five astronauts are going on an extended mission of 72 days in a space station. What is the most efficient way to package their food in a single, solid block? Give the dimensions and the cost of the package.

2. A space team from Jupiter packages their food in a solid block that is $5 \times 12 \times 14$. Is this the most efficient way to package the food? If not, find the most efficient package. If it is, then find the least efficient package. Give the dimensions and surface area of both packages.

Practice Exercises

1. Describe all the different solid blocks that would represent an 18-day supply of food.

   a) List their measures in the table.

BF	BS	H	Volume	Surface Area

   b) Mark the block with the maximum surface area with MAX and the block with the minimum surface area with MIN.

   c) Describe the shapes of the

   MAX _____

   MIN _____

2. Repeat the exercise for a 72-day supply of food and indicate MAX and MIN.

BF	BS	H	Volume	Surface Area

Worksheet 5-4

Practice Exercises

Give the volume and surface area of the blocks below.

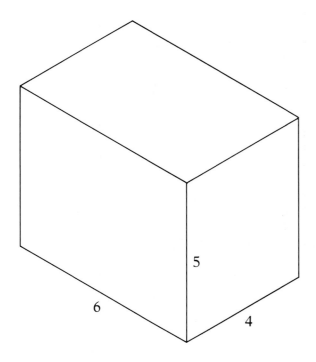

3. Volume = _____

Surface Area = _____

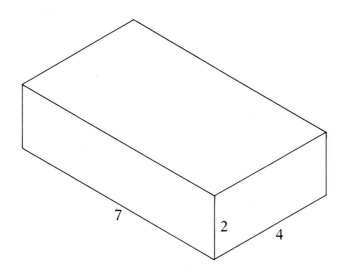

4. Volume = _____

Surface Area = _____

CONSTANT SURFACE AREA— VARYING VOLUME

OVERVIEW

Activity 6 is by far the most difficult of the unit because there are few variations in shapes of solid blocks with a constant surface area, so the directions are more complex. Students are asked to build solid blocks for which the surface area has a ceiling—58 or less—and for which the volume has a floor—more than 14 cubes. Consequently, instead of being able to hold one measure constant while the other varies, both volume and surface area are changing. As a result, some students may think every package must cost $58 or that they must use 14 cubes.

Students generally need assistance in finding a rule for surface area. Highlighting that each face is a rectangle and that faces come in pairs may suffice. Eventually, however, you may have to write down a rule and ask students to verify how it works.

Before students can compare packages in which both volume and surface area change, they need to be introduced to conversion to the relative cost or cost per cube represented by SA/V ratio. Students are encouraged to use calculators in computing these ratios.

Students find the most efficient way to package the food pellets is the most cube-like arrangement, which has the lowest SA/V ratio. Similarly, the least efficient way is the most elongated arrangement, which has the highest SA/V. For packages with the same surface area, the most cube-like arrangement always produces the maximum volume; the most elongated arrangement always produces the minimum. Under some constraints, this pattern might be slightly modified.

Goals for students

1. Measure and record dimensions, volume, and surface area of solid blocks made of cubes by counting or applying the volume rule.

2. Use cubes to form all solid blocks with space armor or surface area constraints (maximum of 22 or 58) and minimum volume (1 or more than 14).

3. Discover and apply rules to measure volume: $V = BF \times BS \times H$; and surface area: $SA = [(BF \times BS) + (BF \times H) + (BS \times H)] \times 2$.

4. Describe food packages with varying costs and volumes by the cost per cube, the SA/V ratio, in order to compare cost efficiency of wrapping packages.

5. Discover and apply the effect of shape on solid blocks with a constant or constrained surface area: volume varies; maximum volume is found in more cube-like solids with minimum SA/V; minimum volume is found in more elongated solids with maximum SA/V.

Materials

2-cm cubes (24 per student).
Calculators.

Worksheets

*6-1, Surface Area Constraints Record Sheet.
 6-2, Extra Challenge.
 6-3, Practice Exercises.

Transparencies

Starred item should be made into a transparency.

CONSTANT SURFACE AREA— VARYING VOLUME

TEACHER ACTION	TEACHER TALK	EXPECTED RESPONSE
Ask.	Build a 5 × 1 × 1 package. How many day's food supply in this package?	5
	What is the mathematical name for the number of cubes?	Volume.
	How much does it cost to wrap this package in a space armor jacket?	$22.
	How did you figure the cost?	Count, or (4 × 5) + 2 = 22.
	What is the mathematical name for the cost?	Surface Area.
	Build all the other packages that can be wrapped for $22 or less. Leave each new example on your desk.	Students tend to have trouble understanding the constraint of $22 or less. Some think they have to spend all $22. Encourage them to find the additional six packages.

BF	BS	H	Volume	S.A.
1	1	1	1	6
2	1	1	2	10
3	1	1	3	14
4	1	1	4	18
2	1	2	4	16
5	1	1	5	22
3	1	2	6	22

TEACHER ACTION	TEACHER TALK	EXPECTED RESPONSE
Collect students' data and record.	What packages did you find? Give me the dimensions, volume, and surface area.	
Pass out Worksheet 6-1. Ask. Give rapid yes/no feedback.	Build a 1 × 14 × 1 package, meaning BF = 1, BS = 14, H = 1. How many day's food supply is it? How much does it cost to package it?	14 days. $58.
Offer students this challenge.	Find all the different packages of more than 14 food pellets without spending more than $58. You can spend less than $58 on a package, but not more.	

OBSERVATIONS	POSSIBLE RESPONSES
Students often think they must spend $58 rather than spend a maximum of $58.	Remind students that $58 is the maximum, and a package can cost less than $58 as long as they package more than 14 cubes.
Students may stop without finding all the possibilities.	There are twelve possibilities.
As an extra challenge, pass out Worksheet 5-2.	

Activity 6 *Summarize*

TEACHER ACTION	TEACHER TALK	EXPECTED RESPONSE

			BF	BS	H	Vol	SA	SA/V
Begin recording the first example.	We began with a 1 × 14 × 1 package, which had a volume of 14 and a surface area of 58.		1	14	1	14	58	4.14
Ask and record. The order of recording depends on student response. The SA/V column will be completed later.	There are twelve ways to have *more* than 14 cubes that cost $58 or less. Who has a different one?		1	2	8	16	52	3.25
			1	2	9	18	58	3.22
			1	3	5	15	46	3.07
Continue until all thirteen are displayed.			1	3	6	18	54	3.00
			1	4	4	16	48	3.00
			1	4	5	20	58	2.90
			2	2	4	16	40	2.50
			2	2	5	20	48	2.40
			2	2	6	24	56	2.33
			2	3	3	18	40	2.22
			2	3	4	24	52	2.17
			3	3	3	27	54	2.00

TEACHER ACTION	TEACHER TALK	EXPECTED RESPONSE
Ask.	Do you see a pattern for finding volume?	$BF \times BS \times H = V$.
	Do you see a pattern for finding surface area?	If no one can see a pattern, use examples from the table.
Ask. Verify the patterns with several examples from the table.	$[(BF \times BS) + (BF \times H) + (BS \times H)] \times 2$. Does this rule work?	Yes.
Extend the lesson by asking students to apply the rules.	Find the surface area and volume of a solid block that is 10 × 2 × 15.	Surface Area = 400 squares. Volume = 300 cubes.
	Find the surface area and volume of a solid block that is 12 × 5 × 20.	Surface Area = 800; $V = 1200$.
	Find the surface area and volume of a solid block that is 3 × 7 × 8.	Surface Area = 202; $V = 168$.

74

Activity 6 *Summarize*

Copyright © 1986 Addison-Wesley Publishing Company, Inc.

TEACHER ACTION	TEACHER TALK	EXPECTED RESPONSE
Ask.	In the first example we had a package of food for 14 days. It cost us $58 for the package, but what did it cost us each day?	$4.14
	How did you find it?	$58 \div 14 = \$4.14$
Record this by adding an SA/V column to the table.	Label the last column SA/V. It tells the cost per day. Record $4.14.	
Have groups calculate SA/V for each cube, using the calculators.	Use your calculators and find the cost per cube for each of your packages.	
Ask and record.	What is the cost of a 1-day food supply in the other packages?	See table above.
Ask.	What is the most economical package? What is its shape?	$3 \times 3 \times 3$ It is a cube with SA/V = 2.0.
	What is the least economical package? What is its shape?	$1 \times 14 \times 1$ It is long and narrow with SA/V = 4.14.
Ask.	If you wanted to package something in the most economical way, what shape would you make the package?	The most cube-like.
	If you wanted to use the most surface area per cube, what shape would you make the package?	The most elongated.
Extend the lesson.	How would you design the most economical package of at least five cubes without spending more than $24 for space armor to wrap the package?	
	Give the dimensions and volume.	$2 \times 2 \times 2 = 8$ cubes; SA = 24.
Assign Worksheet 6-3.	What is one way to send a 12-day supply of food? What is the cost and the SA/V?	$2 \times 2 \times 3 = 12$ cubes; SA = $32

Surface Area Constraints
Record Sheet

BF	BS	H	Volume	Surface Area	

Extra Challenge

1. What is the maximum number of day's worth of food you can package for $200? Give the dimensions, volume, and SA/V ratio.

2. What is the maximum number of day's worth of food you can package for $300? Give the dimensions, volume, and SA/V ratio.

Practice Exercises

1. Listed below are the 21 additional ways to stock up to 12 day's supply of space food. Calculate the space armor cost of each. When there is more than one way to package food for some days, indicate the maximum cost (MAX) and the minimum cost (MIN).

Volume	SA Cost	SA/V	Volume	SA Cost	SA/V
1 day			8 days		
1 × 1 × 1			1 × 1 × 8		
2 days			1 × 2 × 4		
1 × 1 × 2			2 × 2 × 2		
3 days			9 days		
1 × 1 × 3			1 × 1 × 9		
4 days			1 × 3 × 3		
1 × 1 × 4			10 days		
1 × 2 × 2			1 × 1 × 10		
5 days			1 × 2 × 5		
1 × 1 × 5			11 days		
6 days			1 × 1 × 11		
1 × 1 × 6			12 days		
1 × 2 × 3			1 × 1 × 12		
7 days			1 × 2 × 6		
1 × 1 × 7			1 × 3 × 4		

2. **a)** Of all these packages, which is more efficient in terms of SA/V?

   _____ with SA/V = _____

   b) Which package is least efficient in terms of SA/V?

   _____ with SA/V = _____

3. What is the maximum number of day's worth of food you could take for $100?

   BF = _____   BS = _____   H = _____   with SA/V = _____

Activity 7

GROWING SQUARES

Copyright © 1986 Addison-Wesley Publishing Company, Inc.

OVERVIEW

In this activity students encounter growth relationships for the first time. The challenge is to build squares with increasingly large edges and to record their areas and perimeters. The story is that one tile is a square on its first birthday, so the edges are identified with ages. From the data, students are able to discover rules for area and perimeter of squares.

Then students use graph paper to cut out models of their squares and use the models to find the number of smaller squares required to cover a larger square exactly. This data is collected, organized, and displayed so the growth relationship can be seen; as the age, or edge, grows by a factor of n, so does the perimeter. The area grows by a factor of n squared.

Goals for students

1. Learn story interpretation of mathematics: An n-square is a square with an edge of n which is also called an n-year-old square or a square on its nth birthday.

2. Use tiles to build and measure area and perimeter of squares from ages one to six.

3. Find the area and perimeter of squares of specified edges.

4. Cut models of squares with edges 1 to 10, 12, 14, 16, 18, 20, and 21.

5. Discover and apply rules for measuring squares: Area: $A = e^2$ or $e \times e$; Perimeter: $P = e \times 4$.

6. Determine the number of small squares needed to cover a large square exactly by covering and counting.

7. Discover and apply the relationship of growth to squares: If a small square grows to be a large square whose edge is n times as large, then the area grows to be n^2 times as large, and the perimeter grows to be n times as large.

Materials

One-inch tiles (24 per student).

One sheet of graph paper per student.

*Number of Small Squares in a Large Square (Materials 7-1).

Worksheets

*7-1, Growing Squares Record Sheet.

7-2, N-Square Sheet.

7-3, Practice Exercises.

Transparencies

Starred items should be made into transparencies.

GROWING SQUARES

TEACHER ACTION	TEACHER TALK	EXPECTED RESPONSE
Pass out tiles and Worksheet 7-1.		
Display one square and ask.	This is a square on its first birthday. We call it a one-year old square. What is its area? What is its perimeter?	$A = 1$ $P = 4$
Give rapid yes/no feedback.	Show me a square on its second birthday.	▦ Correct ▢ Incorrect
Ask.	What is the area of a two-year-old square? What is the perimeter of a two-year-old square?	$A = 4$ $P = 8$
Ask and record.	How long is the edge of a two-year-old square? What is the perimeter? What is the area? What are the measures for a one-year-old square?	Edge <table><tr><td>Age</td><td>P</td><td>A</td></tr><tr><td>1</td><td>4</td><td>1</td></tr><tr><td>2</td><td>8</td><td>4</td></tr><tr><td>3</td><td>12</td><td>9</td></tr></table>
Repeat the questions and record data for a three-year-old square.		
Provide students with graph paper and offer them this challenge.	Find and record the perimeters and areas of the growing squares indicated on your record sheet. Cut out models and record the age on each square.	

Activity 7 *Explore*

OBSERVATIONS

Students often cut out rectangle models that are close to square (such as 5 × 6).

As the students cut out the various sized squares, you should display one set on a board or wall. The display as shown is necessary for the summary.

A complete set includes 1 to 10, 12-, 14-, 15-, 16-, 18-, 20-, and 21-year-old squares.

As an extra challenge, assign the task of cutting the larger models to those students who complete the first ten most quickly. Squares of ages 12, 14, 15, 16, 18, 20, and 21 are needed by each group in the summary.

POSSIBLE RESPONSES

You can suggest that students test the square by folding the square on its diagonal to see whether the two halves match.

3

7

2

5

4

6

9

8

12

10

14

15

18

16

20

21

TEACHER ACTION	TEACHER TALK	EXPECTED RESPONSE
Collect data and continue recording ages in order.	What is the data for a four-year old square?	

Edge Age	P	A
1	4	1
2	8	4
3	12	9
4	16	16
5	20	25
6	24	36
7	28	49
8	32	64
9	36	81
10	40	100

Continue for ages five to ten.

Ask.

What patterns or rules do you see?

Perimeters increase by 4. Area increases faster.

Record the rules on the board.

$\text{Area} = \text{edge} \times \text{edge}$, or e^2
$\text{Perimeter} = e \times 4$.

Verify the rules with several examples from the table.

Ask.

What will the perimeter and area be for a twelve-year old square?

Continue for squares 12–21.

Edge Age	P	A
12	48	144
14	56	196
15	60	225
16	64	256
18	72	324
20	80	400
21	84	441

Activity 7 *Summarize*

TEACHER ACTION	TEACHER TALK	EXPECTED RESPONSE
Pass out Worksheet 7-2. Ask.	Pick up a two-square and a four-square. How many two-squares can fit in a four-square without overlapping?	4. Have students demonstrate to those who have trouble.
	How many two-squares can fit in a six-square without overlapping?	9.
	How many two-squares can fit in an eight-square?	16.
	Record these results on Worksheet 7-2.	
	Use your squares to find the rest of the answers.	Each group should have the complete set of squares shown in the display.
Display a transparency of Number of Small Squares in a Large Square (Materials 7-1). Ask.	We have been finding how many small squares fit in a large square. What is the smallest number you found?	4.
Gather data and record.	Which pairs of squares require four small squares to make the large square? I will write the size of the smaller square first and the larger square second.	

4	9	16	25	36
2,4	2,6	2,8	2,10	2,12
3,6	3,9	3,12	3,15	3,18
4,8	4,12	4,16	4,20	
5,10	5,15	5,20		
6,12	6,18			
7,14	7,21			

49	64	81	100
2,14	2,16	2,18	2,20
3,21			

TEACHER ACTION		
Gather data and record for succeeding values: 9, 16, 25, 36, 49, 64, 81, and 100.		

TEACHER ACTION	TEACHER TALK	EXPECTED RESPONSE
Point to data and ask.	How are the small and large squares related when there are four small squares in a large square?	The edge of the large squares is twice the edge of the small square.
Repeat for 9, 16, 25, 49, 64, 81, and 100.		The edge of the large square is 3, 4, 5, 6, , 7, 8, 9, and 10 times the edge of the small square.
Ask.	Can you give a general rule for finding how many small squares are needed to exactly cover a large square?	Find the multiple of the edge of the small square and square it, or find what factor the age of the small square is of the large square and square it.
Verify the rule.	Does it work? Check it with some examples.	
Ask.	How many eight-squares in a 24-square? Why?	The edge is 3 times as large, so there are 3×3 or 9 squares.
	How many six-squares in a 24-square?	16.
	If a 40-square has 16 small squares, what is the age of a small square?	10.
	If a 40-square has 64 small squares, what is the age of the small square?	5.
Assign Worksheet 7-3.		

Number of Small Squares in a Large Square

4

_____
_____
_____
_____
_____
_____

9

_____
_____
_____
_____
_____
_____

16

_____
_____
_____
_____
_____
_____

25

_____
_____
_____
_____
_____

36

_____
_____
_____
_____
_____

49

_____
_____
_____
_____
_____

64

_____
_____
_____
_____
_____

81

_____
_____
_____
_____
_____

100

_____
_____
_____
_____
_____
_____

Growing Squares Record Sheet

Square

Edge	Perimeter	Area
1		
2		
3		
4		
5		
6		
7		
8		
9		
10		

N-Square Sheet

Place the small square on the large square to determine the number of small squares it takes to cover the large square exactly.

1. There are ____4____ 2-squares in a 4-square.

2. There are _____ 2-squares in a 6-square.

3. There are _____ 2-squares in an 8-square.

4. There are _____ 2-squares in a 10-square.

5. There are _____ 2-squares in a 12-square.

6. There are _____ 2-squares in a 14-square.

7. There are _____ 2-squares in a 16-square.

8. There are _____ 2-squares in an 18-square.

9. There are _____ 2-squares in a 20-square.

10. There are _____ 3-squares in a 6-square.

11. There are _____ 3-squares in a 9-square.

12. There are _____ 3-squares in a 12-square.

13. There are _____ 3-squares in a 15-square.

14. There are _____ 3-squares in an 18-square.

15. There are _____ 3-squares in a 21-square.

16. There are _____ 4-squares in an 8-square.

17. There are _____ 4-squares in a 12-square.

18. There are _____ 4-squares in a 16-square.

19. There are _____ 4-squares in a 20-square.

20. There are _____ 5-squares in a 10-square.

21. There are _____ 5-squares in a 15-square.

22. There are _____ 5-squares in a 20-square.

23. There are _____ 6-squares in a 12-square.

24. There are _____ 6-squares in an 18-square.

25. There are _____ 7-squares in a 14-square.

26. There are _____ 7-squares in a 21-square.

Practice Exercises

1. A checkerboard is an 8-square.

    a) How many separate 4-squares can you cut from an 8-square? _____

    b) How many separate 2-squares can you cut from an 8-square? _____

    c) How many separate 1-squares can you cut from an 8-square? _____

2. What size square will hold 36 2-squares? _____

3. What size square will hold 49 3-squares? _____

4. What size square will hold 100 8-squares? _____

5. A 120-square holds 4 of what size square? _____

Extra Challenge

    a) In problem 1, how would the answers change if you allowed the 4-squares to overlap each other?

    b) What is the total number of squares on a checkerboard? (A checkerboard has an edge of 8.)

Worksheet 7-3

Activity 8

GROWING CUBES

OVERVIEW

In this activity students examine the growth relationships with cubes. Similar to the story used in Activity 7, the single cube is referred to as a cube on its first birthday. As the edge, or age, of the cube grows, the students build models and find the measures for volume and surface area. From that data, additional measures can be projected and rules found for the volume and surface area of cubes.

Students can avoid the frustration of having large cubes collapse and blocks fall on the floor if they build their models on the floor. To reduce the time needed to build every model, students are assigned only one larger model to build and asked to move from model to model to obtain their measures.

During this activity, the growth relationships are used to solve the Mouse and Elephant questions. Through careful display and examination of data, students find that as the edge of a cube grows by a factor of n, the volume grows by a factor of n cubed, and the surface area grows by a factor of n squared. By viewing the elephant as a 40-year-old mouse, students can figure 64,000 mice are needed on the scale to balance the elephant. A simplified pattern based on the number of mouse coats rather than on the actual surface area makes the second question easier to answer. It takes 1,600 mouse coats to sew a coat for the elephant.

You will want to use your own discretion as to whether the students may use tiles and cubes for the review problems and for the unit test.

Goals for students

1. Learn the story interpretations of mathematics: An n-cube is a cube with an edge of n, which is also called an n-year-old cube or a cube on its nth birthday.
2. Use cubes to build and measure the volume and surface area of cubes from ages one to six.
3. Measure volume and surface area of cubes of specified edges.
4. Discover and apply rules for measuring cubes—Volume: $V = e^3$ or $e \times e \times e$; Surface Area $= SA = e^2 \times 6$.
5. Discover and apply the relationship of growth on cubes: If a small cube grows to be a large cube whose edges are n times as large, then the volume grows to be n^3 times as large, and the surface grows to be n^2 times as large.
6. Solve the Mouse and Elephant questions.

Materials

2-cm cubes (24 per student).

Calculators.

One jacket for a single cube.

Worksheets

*8-1, Growing Cubes Record Sheet.

8-2, Practice Sheet.

Transparencies

Starred item should be made into a transparency.

GROWING CUBES

TEACHER ACTION	TEACHER TALK	EXPECTED RESPONSE
Pass out cubes and Worksheet 8-1.		
Ask. Give rapid yes/no feedback.	This is a cube on its first birthday. Show me a cube on its second birthday.	Correct response Incorrect responses
Ask and record.	How many one-year old cubes does it take to make a two-year-old cube?	8.
Ask and record.	What is the surface area of a one-year-old cube? What would it cost to cover it? What is the surface area of a two-year-old cube? What would it cost to cover it?	6. $6. 24. $24.
Ask. Repeat the questions for a two-year-old cube.	How long is the edge of a one-year-old cube? What is the volume? What is the surface area? Record on Worksheet 8-1.	Edge/Age, V, SA table: Age 1, V 1, SA 6; Age 2, V 8, SA 24
Students need 27 cubes. If not available, have students build in pairs. Give yes/no feedback.	Show me a cube on its third birthday.	
Ask and record.	What is the volume? What is the surface area?	E 3, V 27, SA 54

TEACHER ACTION

Building a four-year-old cube requires cubes from three students.

Gather data and record.

Because of limited time and cubes, designate groups to build the five-year-old and six-year-old cubes. A five-year-old cube requires 6 bags of cubes and a six-year-old cube requires nine bags of cubes.

TEACHER TALK

At your table, share your cubes and build one four-year old cube. Find the volume and surface area. Record them on your record sheet.

What did you find for the volume and surface area?

Build a five- or six-year-old cube as assigned. Record your data, then move to the other cubes. Obtain the data from each cube and record it.

EXPECTED RESPONSE

E	V	SA
...	.	.
4	64	96

OBSERVATIONS

If large cubes are built on the floor initially, they don't fall so often.

As an extra challenge, find data for seven-, eight-, and nine-year-old cubes. Allow students to build one seven-year-old cube, which is 343 cubes.

POSSIBLE RESPONSES

Activity 8 *Summarize*

TEACHER ACTION	TEACHER TALK	EXPECTED RESPONSE
Have students put away cubes. Complete recording the data in order. Mouse coat data is collected later.	What is the new data?	

Edge Age	V	SA	Number of mouse coats
1	1	6	1
2	8	24	4
3	27	54	9
4	64	96	16
5	125	150	25
6	216	216	36

TEACHER ACTION	TEACHER TALK	EXPECTED RESPONSE
Ask. Verify responses.	What is a rule to find volume? Does it work with different aged cubes?	$V = $ edge $\times$ edge $\times$ edge or e^3; yes.
	What is a rule to find surface area? Why? Does this rule work?	$SA = ($edge $\times$ edge$) \times 6$ or $e^2 \times 6$. Six faces with each face a square; yes.
Ask. Record data.	If we built a ten-year-old cube, what would the volume and surface area be?	

E	V	SA
10	1000	600

TEACHER ACTION	TEACHER TALK	EXPECTED RESPONSE
	What is the volume and surface area of a twelve-year-old cube? What about a fifteen-year-old cube? What is the volume and surface area for a twenty-year-old cube?	

E	V	SA
12	1728	864
15	3375	1350
20	8000	2400

94

Activity 8   *Summarize*

TEACHER ACTION	TEACHER TALK	EXPECTED RESPONSE
Ask.	If a one-year-old cube is like a one-year-old mouse and a two-year-old cube is like a two-year-old mouse, how many one-year-old mice will it take to balance a two-year-old mouse?	8.
Repeat the question for three, four, five, 10, 20, and 40.		27, 64, 125, 1000, 8000, and 64,000.
Ask.	What rule tells you how many one-year-old mice it takes to balance an n-year-old mouse? Why?	n^3 or $n \times n \times n$; assuming weights compare like volumes, then the volume rule works.
Ask.	If a one-year-old cube is our mouse, what aged cube is our elephant? Why?	40 years old; the mouse is 6 cm high, the elephant is 240 cm high, or 40 times as large as the mouse.
	So, what is the answer to the mouse and elephant balance question?	64,000.

Activity 8 *Summarize*

TEACHER ACTION	TEACHER TALK	EXPECTED RESPONSE
Display the jacket for a cube and ask.	If a one-year-old cube is a mouse and this jacket is a mouse coat, how much will it cost?	$6.
	How many mouse coats will it take to sew a coat for a two-year-old cube? Why?	4. $24 \div 6 = 4.$
Record.		
	Label the right-hand columns of Worksheet 8-1 with the number of mouse coats and record.	

Edge Age	V	SA	Number of mouse coats
1			1
2			4
3			9
4			16
5			25
10			100
20			400
40			1,600

TEACHER ACTION	TEACHER TALK	EXPECTED RESPONSE
Repeat for three, four, five, 10, 20, and 40.		
Ask.	What rule tells you how many jackets for a one-year-old mouse can be cut from the jacket of an n-year-old mouse? Why?	n^2; it is the pattern in the mouse coat column.
Ask.	If a one-year-old cube is the mouse, what age cube is the elephant?	40.
Check to see whether any student predictions were correct.	How many mouse coats are needed to sew a coat for the elephant?	1,600.
Assign Worksheet 8-2.		

Growing Cubes Record Sheet

Age	Volume	Surface Area	

Practice Sheet

1. a) If a mouse is 5 cm high and an elephant is 250 cm high, how many mice does it take to balance an elephant?

b) How many mouse coats does it take to sew a coat for this elephant?

2. If a seven-foot shark weighs 700 pounds, how much does a 10 foot shark weigh?

3. If a wet suit for a seven-foot shark costs $70, how much is a wet suit for a ten-foot shark?

Worksheet 8-2

Review Problems

1. a) What is the greatest number of people you could seat at a banquet table made from 20 small tables?

b) What is the fewest number of people you could seat?

c) What is the area of your table in each case?

2. a) A banquet table seats 40 people. How many small tables might be required to make the banquet table? List all possibilities.

b) What is the area of each banquet table?

c) Which possibility requires the maximum number of tables?

d) Which possibility requires the minimum number of tables?

Review Problems

3. An astronaut team of four persons is going to spend 12 days in space.

a) How many food cubes do they need?

b) List all the solid block packages of cubes that are possible.

c) What is the space armor jacket cost for each?

d) What is the lowest space armor jacket cost?

e) What is the highest space armor jacket cost?

Review Problems, page 2

Review Problems

4. a) Your space armor budget is $100. Describe some space trips that are possible in terms of the number of astronauts and the number of days.

b) What is the greatest number of people you could take on a one-day trip?

c) What is the longest trip possible?

d) What is the most food you can take?

e) What is the most efficient package in terms of the SA/V ratio?

5. a) How many two-year old squares are required to make a
six-year-old square?

b) Compare the perimeter of a six-year old square to that of a
two-year-old square.

6. a) How many two-year-old cubes are needed to make a
six-year-old cube?

b) Compare the surface area of a two-year-old cube to that of a
six-year-old cube.

7. A balloon that is 4 inches across has 50 square inches of surface
area and 33 cubic inches of air. How much surface area and how
much volume will it have when it is 8 inches across?

NAME

Unit Test

1. For the rectangle at the right, 15 is a measure of _____.

    A area
    B surface area
    C volume
    D perimeter

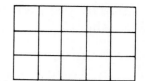

2. The surface area of the solid block shown at the right is _____.

    A 12
    B 19
    C 26
    D 38

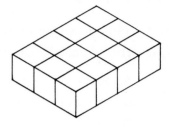

3. The number of people seated at the banquet table is the measure of the _____.

    A area
    B surface area
    C volume
    D perimeter

4. The cost of the space armor jacket needed to wrap the space food is the measure of the _____.

    A area
    B surface area
    C volume
    D perimeter

5. The perimeter of the rectangle at the right is _____.

    A 14
    B 18
    C 22
    D 28

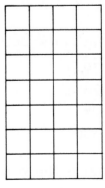

6. The number of day's supply of space food is the measure of the _____.

    A area

    B surface area

    C volume

    D perimeter

7. The number of little tables needed to make a banquet table is the measure of the _____.

    A area

    B surface area

    C volume

    D perimeter

8. For a solid block with dimensions $BF = 2$, $BS = 3$, and $H = 1$, 6 is the measure of _____.

    A area

    B surface area

    C volume

    D perimeter

9. The dimensions of a package of food pellets that the space armor jacket at the right will cover is _____.

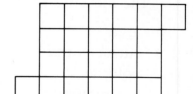

    A $1 \times 4 \times 5$

    B $1 \times 1 \times 5$

    C $1 \times 1 \times 3$

    D $2 \times 2 \times 5$

10. What is the perimeter of a rectangle with dimensions 24×15?

    A 39

    B 74

    C 78

    D 360

11. What is the volume of the solid block shown at the right?

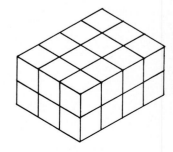

    A 18

    B 24

    C 26

    D 52

12. A rectangular field with an area of 240 has one edge of 20 and the other edge of _____ .

    A 12

    B 100

    C 120

    D 220

13. The surface area of a cube with an edge of 10 is _____ .

    A 60

    B 100

    C 600

    D 1000

14. Which of the following rectangles has a perimeter of 20?

    A *B* of 4 and *S* of 5

    B *B* of 4 and *S* of 6

    C *B* of 8 and *S* of 12

    D *B* of 10 and *S* of 10

15. One square of carpet costs $10. How much does it cost to carpet a room represented by this rectangle?

    A $ 80

    B $ 90

    C $180

    D $200

16. How should you package 40 cubes to obtain the minimum surface area?

    A $5 \times 8 \times 1$

    B $2 \times 4 \times 5$

    C $1 \times 4 \times 10$

    D $1 \times 1 \times 40$

17. A rectangle with a perimeter of 20 will have the maximum area with dimensions of _____ .

    A 4×5

    B 1×20

    C 5×5

    D 1×9

Unit Test

18. Which of the following jackets will not cover the package at the right?

A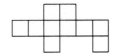

C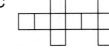

B

D

19. For the solid block shown at the right the volume is _____.

   A 240

   B 168

   C 116

   D   41

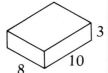

20. A square with a perimeter of 20 has an area of _____.

   A 20

   B 25

   C 40

   D 100

21. The surface area of the solid block shown at the right is _____.

   A 21

   B 47

   C 60

   D 94

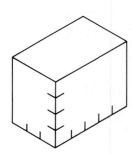

22. You can carry the most space food for the least money in a package measuring _____.

   A $3 \times 8 \times 1$

   B $2 \times 2 \times 4$

   C $2 \times 2 \times 6$

   D $4 \times 1 \times 4$

Unit Test

23. The minimum perimeter for a rectangle with an area of 40 is _____ .

   A 19
   B 26
   C 40
   D 44

24. If a piece of string will go around a square with an edge of 8 exactly once, how many times will it go around a square with an edge of 2?

   A   4
   B   6
   C   8
   D 16

25. If you cut a square with an edge of 18 into smaller squares, each with an edge of 2, how many two-squares will you have?

   A   9
   B 16
   C 36
   D 81

26. There is enough space armor in a jacket for a cube with an edge of 8 to make jackets for how many cubes with an edge of 2?

   A   4
   B   6
   C 16
   D 64

27. If you break a cube with an edge of 8 into cubes with edges of 2, how many two-cubes will you have?

   A 64
   B 16
   C   6
   D   4

Unit Test

28. A box of popcorn sells for 40¢. If you want to sell a smaller box one half as large in each dimension, what is a fair price to charge for the smaller box?

  A   5¢
  B   10¢
  C   20¢
  D   25¢

29. You have a melon in your garden that is three inches across. If it grows to be six inches across, how many times larger is the rind of the 6-inch melon than the 3-inch melon?

  A   2
  B   4
  C   6
  D   8

30. If the 3-inch melon weighs 3 ounces, what would the 6-inch melon weigh?

  A   6
  B   9
  C   12
  D   24

Unit Test Answer Sheet

1.	A	B	C	D		**16.**	A	B	C	D
2.	A	B	C	D		**17.**	A	B	C	D
3.	A	B	C	D		**18.**	A	B	C	D
4.	A	B	C	D		**19.**	A	B	C	D
5.	A	B	C	D		**20.**	A	B	C	D
6.	A	B	C	D		**21.**	A	B	C	D
7.	A	B	C	D		**22.**	A	B	C	D
8.	A	B	C	D		**23.**	A	B	C	D
9.	A	B	C	D		**24.**	A	B	C	D
10.	A	B	C	D		**25.**	A	B	C	D
11.	A	B	C	D		**26.**	A	B	C	D
12.	A	B	C	D		**27.**	A	B	C	D
13.	A	B	C	D		**28.**	A	B	C	D
14.	A	B	C	D		**29.**	A	B	C	D
15.	A	B	C	D		**30.**	A	B	C	D

Area and Perimeter

NAME _____

Figure 1
Area __12__
Perimeter __14__

Figure 2
Area __4__
Perimeter __10__

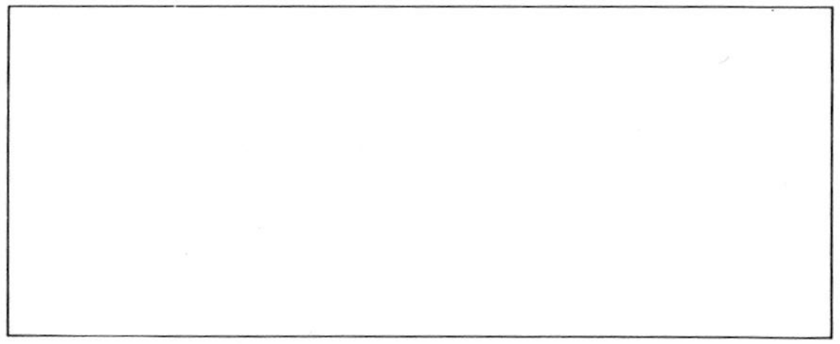

Figure 3
Area __10__
Perimeter __14__

Worksheet 1-2

14

Rectangle Measures

NAME _____

Figure A
Area __8__
Perimeter __12__

Figure B
Area __7__
Perimeter __16__

Figure C
Area __9__
Perimeter __12__

Worksheet 1-1

13

111

Answers

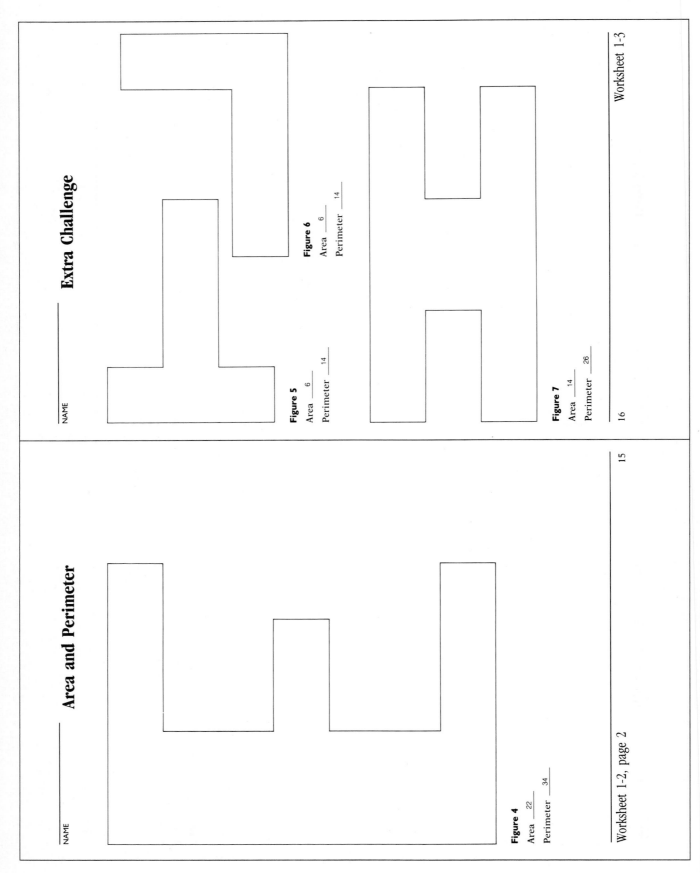

NAME

Extra Challenge

Figure 5
Area ___6___
Perimeter ___14___

Figure 6
Area ___6___
Perimeter ___14___

Figure 7
Area ___14___
Perimeter ___26___

16

Worksheet 1-3

NAME

Area and Perimeter

Figure 4
Area ___22___
Perimeter ___34___

Worksheet 1-2, page 2   15

Copyright © 1986 Addison-Wesley Publishing Company, Inc.

Answers

Practice Exercises

NAME _____

1. $A =$ ___7___ $P =$ ___16___

2. $A =$ ___5___ $P =$ ___12___

3. Draw in separate squares to give an area of 9, then find the perimeter.

$P =$ ___20___

4. Draw in separate squares to give a perimeter of 18, then find the area.

$A =$ ___10___

5. Add a square so that the area is 6 and the perimeter is still 12.

6. Add squares so that the perimeter is 18. What is the new area?

$A =$ ___8___

Various answers; shown is one example.

18

Worksheet 1-4

Constant Area Record Sheet

NAME _____

| Dimensions | | Area | Perimeter |
Bottom Edge	Side Edge	Number of Tables	Number of People
1	24	24	50
2	12	24	28
3	8	24	22
4	6	24	20
6	4	24	20
8	3	24	22
12	2	24	28
24	1	24	50

25

Worksheet 2-1

Answers

NAME _____

Practice Exercises

You will need a sheet of grid paper.

1. On the grid paper, draw *all* possible banquet tables that can be made in the shape of a rectangle using 18 small tables (tiles). Give the area and perimeter of each banquet table.

1×18: $A = 38$ $P = 38$

2×9: $A = 18$ $P = 22$

3×6: $A = 18$ $P = 18$

2. a) Of the banquet tables you found in problem 1, which table will seat the greatest number of people? What are its dimensions?

$B = \underline{18}$ $S = \underline{1}$ $P = \underline{38}$

b) Which of the tables from problem 1 will seat the fewest number of people?

$B = \underline{6}$ $S = \underline{3}$ $P = \underline{18}$

3. a) Use the same procedure as in problem 1 but with 72 small tables. Which rectangle would have the greatest perimeter?

$B = \underline{72}$ $S = \underline{1}$ $P = \underline{146}$

b) Which rectangle would have the smallest perimeter?

$B = \underline{9}$ $S = \underline{8}$ $P = \underline{34}$

Worksheet 2-3

27

NAME _____

Extra Challenge

1. If you had 100 small tables to make into a banquet table, what is the greatest number of people you could seat at the banquet table?

Greatest _____ 202 _____ with $B = $ _____ 100 _____ and $S = $ _____ 1 _____

What is the fewest number of people you could seat at the banquet table?

Fewest _____ 40 _____ with $B = $ _____ 10 _____ and $S = $ _____ 10 _____

2. What if you had 200 small tables to make into a banquet table?

Greatest _____ 402 _____ with $B = $ _____ 200 _____ and $S = $ _____ 1 _____

Fewest _____ 60 _____ with $B = $ _____ 20 _____ and $S = $ _____ 10 _____

3. If you had 90 small tables, what arrangement would seat the fewest number of people at the banquet table?

Fewest _____ 38 _____ with $B = $ _____ 10 _____ and $S = $ _____ 9 _____

What arrangement would seat the greatest number of people at the banquet table?

Greatest _____ 182 _____ with $B = $ _____ 90 _____ and $S = $ _____ 1 _____

4. If you had 1,144 small tables, what arrangement would seat the greatest number of people?

Greatest: Arrangement _____ $1{,}144 \times 1$ _____ People _____ 2,290 _____

What arrangement would seat the fewest number of people?

Fewest: Arrangement _____ 44×26 _____ People _____ 140 _____

Worksheet 2-2

26

Copyright © 1986 Addison-Wesley Publishing Company, Inc.

114

Answers

Constant Perimeter Record Sheet

NAME

Dimensions		Perimeter	Area
B	S		
1	11	24	11
2	10	24	20
3	9	24	27
4	8	24	32
5	7	24	35
6	6	24	36
7	5	24	35
8	4	24	32
9	3	24	27
10	2	24	20
11	1	24	11

Extra Challenge

NAME

1. a) What is the greatest number of tables needed to seat 100 people?

625 (25 × 25)

b) What is the fewest number of tables needed to seat 100 people?

49 (49 × 1)

2. a) What is the greatest number of tables needed to seat 250 people?

3906 (63 × 62)

b) What is the fewest number of tables needed to seat 250 people?

124 (124 × 1)

Answers

116

NAME

Practice Exercises

You will need a sheet of grid paper.

1. On grid paper, draw all the possible banquet tables in the shape of a rectangle that will seat 18 people. Write down the area and perimeter of each banquet table:

1×8, $A = 18$, $P = 18$

2×7, $A = 14$, $P = 18$

3×6, $A = 18$, $P = 18$

4×5, $A = 20$, $P = 18$

2. Using the rectangles you found in problem 1, answer the following questions.

a) What is the fewest number of tables you need?

$A = \underline{\quad 8 \quad}$ with dimensions $B = \underline{\quad 8 \quad}$, $S = \underline{\quad 1 \quad}$

b) What is the greatest number of tables you need?

$A = \underline{\quad 20 \quad}$ with dimensions $B = \underline{\quad 5 \quad}$, $S = \underline{\quad 4 \quad}$

3. a) For a rectangle with perimeter of 72, what rectangle has the largest area?

$A = \underline{\quad 324 \quad}$ with dimensions $B = \underline{\quad 18 \quad}$, $S = \underline{\quad 18 \quad}$

b) What rectangle has the smallest area?

$A = \underline{\quad 35 \quad}$ with dimensions $B = \underline{\quad 35 \quad}$, $S = \underline{\quad 1 \quad}$

Worksheet 3-3

37

NAME

Fixed Perimeter Graph

Worksheet 3-4

38

Answers

Space Food Packages
Record Sheet

NAME

Space food package	Number of days the food supply will last	Cost of space armor jacket	BF	BS	H
A	1	$6	1	1	1
B	2	10	1	2	1
C	3	14	1	3	1
D	4	18	1	4	1
E	4	16	2	2	1
F	6	26	1	6	1
G	6	22	2	3	2
H	8	24	2	2	2
I	8	28	2	4	1
J	8	34	1	8	1

54

Worksheet 4-1

Fixed Area Graph

NAME

39

Worksheet 3-5

117

Answers

NAME

Practice Exercises

Find the number of days the food supply will last, or the volume of each space armor jacket. Also, find the surface area (the cost of the jacket) and the dimensions of the package.

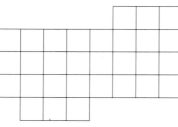

Volume = __6__ Surface Area = __26__

Dimensions = __1__ , __1__ , __6__

Volume = __9__ Surface Area = __30__

Dimensions = __1__ , __3__ , __3__

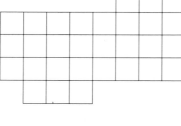

Volume = __16__ Surface Area = __40__

Dimensions = __2__ , __2__ , __4__

Worksheet 4-4

NAME

Extra Challenge

Cut jackets for the food packages illustrated below and find the cost for each:

1. L-shape

$34

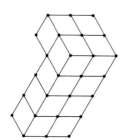

2. Half-cube

$27 + (9 \times \sqrt{2})$

$= 27 + 12.7279$

approx. $39.73

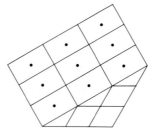

3. Square doughnut

$32

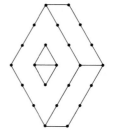

Worksheet 4-3

56

118

Answers

Copyright © 1986 Addison-Wesley Publishing Company, Inc.

Practice Exercises

NAME _____

Some of these space armor jackets cover one cube, some do not.
Circle the numbers of the jackets that *do* cover one cube.

1.

2.

3.

4.

5.

6.

7.

8.

9.

10.

11.

12.

58   Worksheet 4-4, page 2

Solid Blocks

NAME _____

Place 12 cubes on each rectangle.

Rectangle A

Height __2__

Bottom side edge __2__

Bottom front edge __3__

Rectangle B

Height __3__

Bottom side edge __4__

Bottom front edge __1__

Rectangle C

Height __6__

Bottom side edge __1__

Bottom front edge __2__

65   Worksheet 5-1

119

Answers

Constant Volume Record Sheet

Dimensions			Volume	Surface Area
BF	BS	H		
1	1	24	24	98
1	2	12	24	76
1	3	8	24	70
1	4	6	24	68
2	2	6	24	56
2	3	4	24	52

Worksheet 5-2

Extra Challenge

1. A team of five astronauts are going on an extended mission of 72 days in a space station. What is the most efficient way to package their food in a single, solid block? Give the dimensions and the cost of the package.

$5 \times 72 = 360$ cubes

$V = 6 \times 6 \times 10 = 360$ cubes

SA = $312

2. A space team from Jupiter packages their food in a solid block that is $5 \times 12 \times 14$. Is this the most efficient way to package the food? If not, find the most efficient package. If it is, then find the least efficient package. Give the dimensions and surface area of both packages.

No. $5 \times 12 \times 14 = 840$ SA = $596

most efficient $6 \times 10 \times 14 = 840$ SA = $568

least efficient $1 \times 1 \times 840$ SA = $3,362

Worksheet 5-3

Answers

NAME _____

Practice Exercises

1. Describe all the different solid blocks that would represent an 18-day supply of food.

a) List their measures in the table.

BF	BS	H	Volume	Surface Area	
1	1	18	18	74	MAX
1	2	9	18	58	
1	3	6	18	54	
2	3	3	18	42	MIN

b) Mark the block with the maximum surface area with MAX and the block with the minimum surface area with MIN.

c) Describe the shapes of the

MAX long and thin

MIN more cube-like

2. Repeat the exercise for a 72-day supply of food and indicate MAX and MIN.

BF	BS	H	Volume	Surface Area	
1	1	72	72	290	MAX
1	2	36	72	220	
1	3	24	72	198	
1	4	18	72	188	
1	6	12	72	180	
1	8	9	72	178	
2	2	18	72	152	
2	3	12	72	132	
2	4	9	72	124	
2	6	6	72	120	
3	3	8	72	114	
3	4	6	72	108	MIN

Worksheet 5-4

68

NAME _____

Practice Exercises

Give the volume and surface area of the blocks below.

3. Volume = $6 \times 5 \times 4 = 120$

Surface Area = $(30 + 20 + 24) \times 2 = 74 \times 2 = 148$

4. Volume = $4 \times 2 \times 7 = 56$

Surface Area = $(8 + 14 + 28) \times 2 = 50 \times 2 = 100$

Worksheet 5-4, page 2

69

121

Answers

Surface Area Constraints Record Sheet

BF	BS	H	Volume	Surface Area	SA/V
1	14	1	14	58	4.14
1	2	8	16	52	3.25
1	2	9	18	58	3.22
1	3	5	15	46	3.07
1	3	6	18	54	3.00
1	4	4	16	48	3.00
1	4	5	20	58	2.90
2	2	4	16	40	2.50
2	2	5	20	48	2.40
2	2	6	24	56	2.33
2	3	3	18	40	2.22
2	3	4	24	52	2.17
3	3	3	27	54	2.00

Extra Challenge

1. What is the maximum number of day's worth of food you can package for $200? Give the dimensions, volume, and SA/V ratio.

$5 \times 6 \times 6$

$V = 5 \times 6 \times 6 = 180$ day's worth of food

$SA = (30 + 30 + 36) \times 2 = 192$

$SA/V = 1.06666$

Note: Some students may suggest adding 3 more cubes. This would not be a solid block, but would increase the numbers $V = 183$ and $SA = 200$. This is not as good a package because $SA/V = 1.0928962$.

2. What is the maximum number of day's worth of food you can package for $300? Give the dimensions, volume, and SA/V ratio.

$7 \times 7 \times 7$

$SA = 6 \times (7 \times 7) = 294$

$V = 7 \times 7 \times 7 = 343$

$SA/V = .8571429$

Answers

NAME _____

Practice Exercises

1. Listed below are the 21 additional ways to stock up to 12 day's supply of space food. Calculate the space armor cost of each. When there is more than one way to package food for some days, indicate the maximum cost (MAX) and the minimum cost (MIN).

Volume	SA Cost	SA/V		Volume	SA Cost	SA/V
1 day				8 days		
1 × 1 × 1	6	6.00		1 × 1 × 8	34	4.25 MAX
2 days				1 × 2 × 4	28	3.50
1 × 1 × 2	10	5.00		2 × 2 × 2	24	3.00 MIN
3 days				9 days		
1 × 1 × 3	14	4.67		1 × 1 × 9	38	4.22 MAX
4 days				1 × 3 × 3	30	3.33 MIN
1 × 1 × 4	18	4.50 MAX		10 days		
1 × 2 × 2	16	4.00 MIN		1 × 1 × 10	42	4.20 MAX
5 days				1 × 2 × 5	34	3.40 MIN
1 × 1 × 5	22	4.40		11 days		
6 days				1 × 1 × 11	46	4.18
1 × 1 × 6	26	4.33 MAX		12 days		
1 × 2 × 3	22	3.67 MIN		1 × 1 × 12	50	4.17 MAX
7 days				1 × 2 × 6	40	3.33
1 × 1 × 7	30	4.29		1 × 3 × 4	38	3.17 MIN

2. a) Of all these packages, which is more efficient in terms of SA/V?

2 × 2 × 2 with SA/V = 3.00

b) Which package is least efficient in terms of SA/V?

1 × 1 × 1 with SA/V = 6.00

3. What is the maximum number of day's worth of food you could take for $100?

BF = 4   BS = 4   H = 4   with SA/V = $\frac{96}{64}$ = 1.50

NAME _____

Growing Squares Record Sheet

Square

Edge	Perimeter	Area
1	4	1
2	8	4
3	12	9
4	16	16
5	20	25
6	24	36
7	28	49
8	32	64
9	36	81
10	40	100
12	48	144
14	56	196
15	60	225
16	64	256
18	72	324
20	80	400
21	84	441

Answers

N-Square Sheet

Place the small square on the large square to determine the number of small squares it takes to cover the large square exactly.

1. There are **4** 2-squares in a 4-square.
2. There are **9** 2-squares in a 6-square.
3. There are **16** 2-squares in an 8-square.
4. There are **25** 2-squares in a 10-square.
5. There are **36** 2-squares in a 12-square.
6. There are **49** 2-squares in a 14-square.
7. There are **64** 2-squares in a 16-square.
8. There are **81** 2-squares in an 18-square.
9. There are **100** 2-squares in a 20-square.
10. There are **4** 3-squares in a 6-square.
11. There are **9** 3-squares in a 9-square.
12. There are **16** 3-squares in a 12-square.
13. There are **25** 3-squares in a 15-square.
14. There are **36** 3-squares in an 18-square.
15. There are **49** 3-squares in a 21-square.
16. There are **4** 4-squares in an 8-square.
17. There are **9** 4-squares in a 12-square.
18. There are **16** 4-squares in a 16-square.
19. There are **25** 4-squares in a 20-square.
20. There are **4** 5-squares in a 10-square.
21. There are **9** 5-squares in a 15-square.
22. There are **16** 5-squares in a 20-square.
23. There are **4** 6-squares in a 12-square.
24. There are **9** 6-squares in an 18-square.
25. There are **4** 7-squares in a 14-square.
26. There are **9** 7-squares in a 21-square.

Practice Exercises

1. A checkerboard is an 8-square.
   a) How many separate 4-squares can you cut from an 8-square? **4**
   b) How many separate 2-squares can you cut from an 8-square? **16**
   c) How many separate 1-squares can you cut from an 8-square? **64**

2. What size square will hold 36 2-squares? **12 × 12 or 12-square**

3. What size square will hold 49 3-squares? **21-square**

4. What size square will hold 100 8-squares? **80-square**

5. A 120-square holds 4 of what size square? **60-square**

Extra Challenge

a) In problem 1, how would the answers change if you allowed the 4-squares to overlap each other? **25**

b) What is the total number of squares on a checkerboard? (A checkerboard has an edge of 8.)

64 + 49 + 36 + 25 + 16 + 9 + 4 + 1 = 204

Answers

Growing Cubes Record Sheet

NAME

Age	Volume	Surface Area	Mouse Coats
1	1	6	1
2	8	24	4
3	27	54	9
4	64	96	16
5	125	150	25
6	216	216	36
7	343	294	49
8	512	384	64
9	729	486	81
10	1,000	600	100
15	3,375	1,350	225
20	8,000	2,400	400
30	27,000	5,400	900
40	64,000	9,600	1,600

Worksheet 8-1

Practice Sheet

NAME

1. a) If a mouse is 5 cm high and an elephant is 250 cm high, how many mice does it take to balance an elephant?

$(50)^3 = 125,000$

b) How many mouse coats does it take to sew a coat for this elephant?

$(50)^2 = 2,500$

2. If a seven-foot shark weighs 700 pounds, how much does a 10 foot shark weigh?

$\left(\frac{10}{7}\right)^3 \times 700 = 2,040.8$ pounds

3. If a wet suit for a seven-foot shark costs $70, how much is a wet suit for a ten-foot shark?

$\left(\frac{10}{7}\right)^2 \times 70 = \$142.86$

Worksheet 8-2

125

Answers

Review Problems

NAME

3. An astronaut team of four persons is going to spend 12 days in space.

a) How many food cubes do they need?

4 × 12 = 48 cubes

b) List all the solid block packages of cubes that are possible.

1 × 1 × 48	1 × 6 × 8
1 × 2 × 24	2 × 2 × 12
1 × 3 × 16	2 × 3 × 8
1 × 4 × 12	3 × 4 × 4

c) What is the space armor jacket cost for each?

1 × 1 × 48: $194	1 × 6 × 8: $124
1 × 2 × 24: $148	2 × 2 × 12: $104
1 × 3 × 16: $134	2 × 3 × 8: $92
1 × 4 × 12: $128	3 × 4 × 4: $80

d) What is the lowest space armor jacket cost?

3 × 4 × 4

SA = $80 (minimum)

e) What is the highest space armor jacket cost?

1 × 1 × 48

SA = $194 (maximum)

Review Problems

NAME

1. a) What is the greatest number of people you could seat at a banquet table made from 20 small tables?

42

b) What is the fewest number of people you could seat?

18

c) What is the area of your table in each case?

20

2. a) A banquet table seats 40 people. How many small tables might be required to make the banquet table? List all possibilities.

1 × 19	4 × 16	7 × 13	10 × 10
2 × 18	5 × 15	8 × 12	
3 × 17	6 × 14	9 × 11	

b) What is the area of each banquet table?

1 × 19; A = 19	4 × 16; A = 64	7 × 13; A = 91	10 × 10; A = 100
2 × 18; A = 36	5 × 15; A = 75	8 × 12; A = 96	
3 × 17; A = 51	6 × 14; A = 84	9 × 11; A = 99	

c) Which possibility requires the maximum number of tables?

10 × 10 = 100 (maximum)

d) Which possibility requires the minimum number of tables?

1 × 19 = 19 (minimum)

126

Answers

Review Problems

NAME

4. a) Your space armor budget is $100. Describe some space trips that are possible in terms of the number of astronauts and the number of days.

There are many possibilities.

One example: 2 persons for 3 days at a cost of $22.

b) What is the greatest number of people you could take on a one-day trip?

64 people

c) What is the longest trip possible?

One person for 64 days

d) What is the most food you can take?

64 cubes

e) What is the most efficient package in terms of the SA/V ratio?

4 × 4 × 4 = 64 cubes

SA/V = 1.50

Review Problems, page 3

101

Review Problems

NAME

5. a) How many two-year old squares are required to make a six-year-old square?

9

b) Compare the perimeter of a six-year old square to that of a two-year-old square.

6-square, $P = 24$

2-square, $P = 8$

Perimeter is 3 times as large.

6. a) How many two-year-old cubes are needed to make a six-year-old cube?

27

b) Compare the surface area of a two-year-old cube to that of a six-year-old cube.

2-cube, SA = 24

6-cube, SA = 216

Surface area is $\frac{1}{9}$ as large.

7. A balloon that is 4 inches across has 50 square inches of surface area and 33 cubic inches of air. How much surface area and how much volume will it have when it is 8 inches across?

SA = 5 × 2^2 = 200 square inches

V = 33 × 2^3 = 264 cubic inches

Review Problems, page 4

102

127

Unit Test Answer Key

1. A		**16.** B	
2. D		**17.** C	
3. D		**18.** D	
4. B		**19.** A	
5. C		**20.** B	
6. C		**21.** D	
7. A		**22.** C	
8. C		**23.** B	
9. B		**24.** A	
10. C		**25.** D	
11. B		**26.** C	
12. A		**27.** A	
13. C		**28.** A	
14. B		**29.** B	
15. C		**30.** D	